THE LITERACY MAP

GUIDING CHILDREN TO WHERE THEY NEED TO BE

(4-6)

by
J. Richard Gentry

with contributions by
Jean Mann
Lynn Pott
Tony Stead
Margaret Trauernicht

ACKNOWLEDGMENTS

The author and publisher wish to thank those who gave permission to reprint borrowed material. Every effort has been made to trace the ownership of all copyrighted materials in this book and to obtain permission for their use.

Literacy Plus Teacher Reference Book to Words in Semantic Clusters by Robert J. Marzano, Diane Paynter, John S. Kendall, Debra Pickering and Lorraine Marzano. © 1991. Used with permission from Zaner-Bloser, Inc.

Excerpts from *Spell It—Write!* © 1998. Used with permission from Zaner-Bloser, Inc.

From *Literature Circles: Voice and Choice in the Student-Centered Classroom*, by Harvey Daniels. Copyright © 1994. Reprinted by permission from Stenhouse Publishers, Portland, Maine.

Excerpt from *How to Read a Poem and Fall in Love with Poetry*, copyright © 1999 by Edward Hirsch, reprinted by permission of Harcourt, Inc.

Reprinted with the permission of Scribner, a Division of Simon & Schuster, Inc., from *How to Read and Why* by Harold Bloom. Copyright © 2000 by Harold Bloom.

Reprinted with the permission of Simon & Schuster Books for Young Readers, an imprint of Simon & Schuster Children's Publishing Division from *Frindle* by Andrew Clements. Text copyright © 1996 Andrew Clements.

Reprinted with the permission of Atheneum Books for Young Readers, an imprint of Simon & Schuster Children's Publishing Division from *Shiloh* by Phyllis Reynolds Naylor. Copyright © 1991 Phyllis Reynolds Naylor.

Reprinted with the permission of Atheneum Books for Young Readers, an imprint of Simon & Schuster Children's Publishing Division from *Mrs. Frisby and the Rats of NIMH* by Robert C. O'Brien. Copyright © 1971 Robert C. O'Brien; copyright renewed © 1999 Christopher Conly, Jane Leslie Conly, Kane Conly and Sarah Conly.

Excerpts from *Spelling in Use: Looking Closely at Spelling in Whole Language Classrooms* by Lester Laminack and Katie Wood. Copyright © 1996 by the National Council of Teachers of English. Reprinted with permission.

Excerpts from the *West Virginia Instructional Goals and Objectives* reprinted with permission from the West Virginia Department of Education.

Excerpt from *Harcourt Science Grade 3, 2000*, reprinted by permission of Harcourt, Inc.

Continued on page 205

Printed in the United States of America
02 03 04 05 06 07   9 8 7 6 5 4 3 2 1
Edited by Emmi S. Herman
Designed by Harry Chester, Inc.

Library of Congress Cataloging-in-Publication Data
Gentry, J. Richard.
    The literacy map : guiding children to where they need to be (4-6)/by J. Richard Gentry.
        p. cm.
    Includes bibliographical references.
    ISBN 1-59034-188-0 (pbk.)
        1. Language arts (Elementary) I. Title.

LB1576 .G39 2002
372.6—dc21   2001052216

CONTENTS

This book is dedicated to
Bill Boswell

–J.R.G.

THE LITERACY JOURNEY

Over the past two years I have traveled around the country presenting fourth- through sixth-grade teachers the concept that they can follow a "map" to guide children at their grade level to expected literacy outcomes.

One fourth-grade teacher told me she made a subtle shift to focus more on prewriting in her writing workshop. She started emphasizing student-chosen as opposed to teacher-chosen topics. She encouraged writers to spend more time planning and creating a story map, mandating that the plan be turned in along with the edited first draft. A fifth-grade teacher told me he revamped his spelling program, having students do split word lists, adding words they misspell often in their own writing. A sixth-grade teacher made changes in her reading program, adding an extensive reading standard based on the volume of reading that sixth graders should accomplish.

Each of these teachers had a fresh understanding of the map for literacy education at their grade level with its essential elements presented in correct forms, sizes, and relationships. The map presents the whole literacy journey expected by students at a particular grade level and includes successful instructional strategies, models of quality literacy experiences, and interventions for teaching literacy.

Whatever your teaching philosophy may be, there are certain desired learning outcomes expected in the fourth-, fifth-, and sixth-grade classroom. Embrace the concept of a map for literacy for your grade level, and filter it through your own philosophy, values, favorite books, and teaching experience. The map will not limit you in any way or dictate how you teach. Rather, it will provide the structure you need to assess, plan, and teach effectively. The map will help you guide your students where you want them to be and enable you to determine how well you have succeeded.

J. Richard Gentry, Ph.D.

CHAPTER 1

YOU NEED A MAP FOR GRADES FOUR, FIVE, AND SIX

When I wrote *The Literacy Map (K-3)*, I used an analogy—a literacy map is like a map of Chicago. This representation is not the journey itself any more than a map of Chicago is Chicago. It simply makes it easier to get where you want to be. In the same way that the city map is not the physical street, the literacy map is not the curriculum. You must make many important curricula decisions to support the literacy journey for each child.

The concept of the literacy map came to me in 1996 when President Clinton convened the National Education Summit of all 50 governors and 44 top U.S. corporate leaders to aid school reform. The group planned to jumpstart the standards movement by helping states figure out what students should know and be able to do. I applauded this catalyst for reform that brought governors and business leaders together to bring a world-class education system to the U.S. I agreed with their belief that teachers needed clear and specific goals along with a common understanding of the desired learning outcomes for literacy learning at each grade level. I had become quite frustrated with a trend in the 1990s leading many state departments of education and even our own professional organizations to disseminate nebulous K-6 language arts curricula and standards. Those standards lacked the specificity necessary to be useful to teachers or to make sense to parents. Parents want to know whether their children are on grade level. I asked myself the same question the governors were asking: *Couldn't we be more specific and concrete?* I believed teachers needed specific literacy goals at each grade level because a curriculum that is not specifically defined cannot be instructionally supported (Shanahan, 1997).

My experience as a teacher, professor, educational researcher and author gave me confidence that both research and practice had established grade-level literacy benchmarks for what children should know and be able to do. But those were not being well articulated to teachers, parents, politicians, or business leaders. The governors were right: we needed to establish a clear understanding of what should be expected.

But I worried because so few educators were involved at the National Education Summit. That is why I resolved to synthesize the research, to examine how states and local districts were approaching standards, and to write a practical and usable handbook.

As a teacher of literacy you face two challenges. Challenge number one is that you must know the essence of literacy learning—literacy goals or benchmarks—expected of students at your particular grade level. I call this challenge "knowing the map." There should be some common understanding among teachers at a particular grade level of desired learning outcomes for that grade, for example: *What kinds of books match well with readers who function on a particular grade level? When teaching word-specific knowledge, what are the best words or patterns to teach? What should writing look like? How does reading and writing change from fourth-, to fifth-, to sixth-grade levels?* Knowing the map for your grade level will help you assess each child's progress accurately and make the appropriate instructional choices.

Challenge number two is that you must have a thorough understanding of the literacy level of each child in your classroom—you must know each child as a reader, a writer, a speller, a thinker, and a user of words. I call this objective "knowing each child individually." Mapping out literacy for your grade level helps you accomplish this goal.

The literacy maps in this book are constructed with grade-level benchmark checklists that represent minimum acceptable literacy criteria for your grade level. The benchmarks relate to a child's capacity to explore ideas as a reader, writer, speller, and user of words and to acquire and use information. A solid set of benchmarks is specifically defined. Benchmarks help you determine where each child is functioning when he or she begins the year in your classroom, and help you track changes in his or her capacity to acquire literacy and to use information. In part, benchmarks define what you must teach by showing concretely where each child functions in relation to the expected curricula. Achieving benchmarks help children become better readers, writers, and spellers, and help them listen, comprehend, speak, and understand their world.

Teaching is a craft that requires special tools, knowledge, and procedures. *The Literacy Map: Guiding Children to Where They Need to Be (4-6)* contains commentary on classroom management, teaching frameworks, assessment tools, teaching strategies, research synthesis, and practical advice to help fourth- through sixth-grade teachers teach literacy successfully.

The information in this book helps teachers track a student's growth in reading, writing, and spelling. It will also help you to determine whether the readers and writers in your classroom are receiving the quality of instruction they need in order to meet state and local standards and benchmarks or to pass performance-based reading and writing assessments. The literacy maps, scheduling recommendations, instructional strategies, and teaching activities enable you to formulate a plan to help your students meet rigorous standards. The assessment tools allow you to communicate to families how successfully their children are learning.

The literacy maps for grades four through six (pages 147–161) are based on standards and grade-level benchmarks which, at the time of this writing, are required by 45 states. After I wrote *The Literacy Map: Guiding Children to Where They Need to Be (K-3)*, hundreds of middle elementary grade teachers called, wrote, or E-mailed requesting fourth- through sixth-grade literacy maps. This book is designed to meet that need.

The chapters that follow include assessment tools, teaching strategies, and practical advice to help you to provide instructional support, receive feedback, monitor your own successful teaching and most importantly, monitor the literacy growth of each child in your classroom.

Wherever you are on your journey to become the best teacher you can be, the chapters that follow provide a map—with reinforcement, new ideas, encouragement and inspiration, as well as guidelines and practical information to help you along the way.

CHAPTER 2

WHAT SHOULD HAVE HAPPENED BEFORE GRADES FOUR, FIVE, AND SIX

Students who come to you ready for success at your grade-level should be congratulated for the incredible journey to literacy they have made. Four or five or six years ago these children could not read. Most of the children you now teach entered kindergarten with very little knowledge about literacy. When a kindergarten teacher gave them a piece of paper and asked them to write, they probably scribbled. Some knew a few letters of the alphabet but many did not. A few could read words from their environment—*McDonald's, STOP,* or *7-Up*—but some couldn't read any words. Only four, five, or six years ago some of the children now entering your classroom could not read their own names.

Many of the students you now teach had very little concept of how books or words work when they entered kindergarten. Most were not aware of the function of sounds in words and were over a year away from understanding regular phonics patterns or being able to use chunks of letters to read and spell by analogy. Most couldn't spell words accurately or even invent a spelling. Have you ever stopped to think what remarkable achievements they made before walking into your classroom?

In the section that follows, I will describe the way your current fourth-, fifth- and sixth-grade students' initial literacy developed. I will provide a detailed description of how learning to read, write, and spell unfolds to help you shore up your defenses in combating the exigencies of the under-prepared and to help you meet the challenge of teaching children who suffer from learning deficiencies. You need to know what happens at earlier levels of literacy because many of the children you work with have not reached grade-level achievement in some areas.

This chapter will help you:

- Gain a better understanding of what normal literacy development looks like from kindergarten through third grade.
- Make appropriate choices in the type of instruction you choose for children who struggle because their functioning is below grade level.
- Match your instruction to a child's level of functioning.
- Begin to consider the way to manage a class of students of differing abilities.

"LEARNING TO READ AND LEARNING TO SPELL ARE ONE AND THE SAME, ALMOST!"

Inspection of how literacy emerged in your students will show how their reading and spelling development worked together from the very beginning. Learning to invent spelling helps cultivate a child's knowledge of the alphabetic system—the knowledge at the very core of learning to read. A large volume of research supports this view (Ehri, 1997; Gentry, 2000a; Gentry, 2000b; Ehri and Wilce, 1985: Scott and Ehri, 1989; Gough, Juel, and Griffith, 1989; Henderson, 1981). According to researcher Linnea Ehri, "Learning to read and learning to spell are one and the same, almost!" (Ehri, 1997, p. 237). This concept is an important underpinning for the assessment model presented in this book, beginning with inspecting students' writing as a source of evidence for assessing other aspects of literacy. The model has solid grounding in theory and empirical research.

Ehri and other researchers have shown that the same underlying knowledge sources not only support students' reading development, but also their development as writers and spellers (Richgels, 1987, 1995; Ehri, 1997; Gentry, 2000a, 2000b). Reading, writing, and spelling are reciprocal processes. To illustrate this point and better understand emergent literacy, let's take a closer look at the parallel development of early reading and early spelling.

You may be surprised to learn that some of your current students could write before they could read (Chomsky, 1970). It's not a surprising phenomenon once we recognize that what a child knows as a writer and an inventive speller often affects what the child does as an emergent reader. Likewise, what the child does as a reader impacts spelling. The processes of learning to decode and learning to spell dovetail due to their common underlying knowledge sources.

Linnea Ehri's research convincingly shows how the same underlying knowledge sources may fully support both reading and spelling. Look at the way the same underlying knowledge sources support both decoding a word and inventing a spelling in Figure 2.1.

UNLYING KNOWLEDGE SOURCES FOR READING AND SPELLING	
What Children Must Know	**What We Must Teach**
The concept of word	WORDS
How to segment words into sounds	PHONEMIC AWARENESS
How to blend sounds into words	BLENDING
Knowledge of names of the letters	LETTERS
Knowledge of sounds of the letters	SOUNDS
How to group letters into functional units	GRAPHEMES
How these units typically symbolize sounds	PHONICS
How to read and spell words by invention	INVENTED SPELLING
How to read and spell words by analogy	CHUNKING, ONSETS and RIMES PHONICS PATTERNS, SYLLABLES ROOT WORDS, PREFIXES SUFFIXES, ENDINGS
How to read and spell words by memory	WORD-SPECIFIC KNOWLEDGE PERFECT SPELLING

(Adapted form Ehri, 1997)

Figure 2.1

As we review the stages of decoding and invented spelling, we will see that very young children continually revise their theory of how the alphabetic system works and replace what no longer works with new information. Learning to read involves a complex set of attitudes and behaviors. Children use a number of knowledge sources in addition to phonics. Specifically, they use the structure of text and meaning to read. Text structure is important because children use their knowledge of which words sound right together when they read; they are likely to read text like they think it is supposed to sound to them. They expect what they are reading to make sense. In going from the known to the unknown—the basis of all learning—children use their background knowledge and their own experiences to figure out unknown words and to comprehend print.

Attitudes are important; the more children read the better they get at it. So beginning readers need to develop positive attitudes about reading. Not only must children have a lot of opportunity to read, they must want to read. Keep in mind that graphophonics, text structure, meaning, time spent reading, and a child's attitude all impact the success he or she has learning to read.

Both reading and spelling initially develop in stages due to qualitative changes in the way the student thinks letters in words relate to sounds (Gentry, 1982, 2000a, 2000b; Henderson, 1981; Ehri, 1997). Collectively, this knowledge is sometimes referred to as knowledge of the alphabetic system. It includes learning about the concept of word, segmenting sounds in words, recognizing letters, and learning how letters relate to sounds. From the time they enter kindergarten until roughly the end of first grade, students try out four distinct systems for using the English alphabet to read and spell. By the end of first grade they become readers and spellers. Essentially they are using the same system for both reading and spelling that you and I use as literate adults. The four phases, or stages, advance from simple to more complex—from not using an alphabetic system, to partial use, to full use, to consolidated and sophisticated literate adult-like use (Ehri, 1997). Students should have moved up to the fourth stage by the beginning of second grade.

STAGE 1—PRE-ALPHABETIC

Students may enter kindergarten with no recognition of how the alphabet system works. They begin using letters to read and spell arbitrarily or randomly with little or no understanding of the system. This is Stage 1, the pre-alphabetic stage of decoding and invented spelling. At this stage, "children know little about the alphabetic system as it represents speech" (Ehri, 1997, p. 253). Stage 1 shouldn't last very long because children naturally try to make sense of their world. As their concepts of word, knowledge about the alphabet, and knowledge about sounds grow, children's attempts to use the alphabetic system get more sophisticated. They move on to Stage 2.

STAGE 2—PARTIAL ALPHABETIC

At Stage 2, students use a few prominent letters in words to attempt to read and spell. This stage often appears in the second half of kindergarten for students developmentally on track. The alphabetic system begins to make more sense to them as they discover that letters relate to sounds in words, but students function under some limitations. For example, at this point they are not likely to do much chunking of spelling and phonics patterns (Ehri, 1997). As knowledge about letters and sounds grows, young children's strategies for decoding words and for inventing spelling grow in tandem. Stage 2 readers and spellers who make partial use of the alphabetic system move from using some letters to decode and some sounds to invent a spelling to using virtually all the letters to decode and to spelling virtually all the sounds. This is Stage 3.

STAGE 3—FULL ALPHABETIC

Stage 3 is the full alphabetic stage, a benchmark for the middle of first grade. Stage 3 is really quite remarkable for writers. For the first time they can write anything they can say and you can read it. Their invented spellings sometimes look strange. For example, ATE spells *eighty* (name each letter in the sequence, A-T-E) as in ATE PEPLE N A BOS, for *Eighty people in a bus* (a Stage 3 phonetic spelling).

By the middle of first grade, students are learning to read and spell by analogy and by using phonics. As the year progresses they learn to chunk more spelling patterns in words, using knowledge of word families (*f-at, b-at, c-at, r-at, sc-at*). As decoders they put their growing knowledge of regular phonics patterns to use. By two-thirds of the first-grade year, students should have a solid foundation in phonics, having been introduced to approximately 45 letter/sound correspondences that have a utility rate high enough to justify instruction (Burmeister, 1975). Thus, the basic underlying phonics knowledge for reading is learned by two-thirds of the first-grade year. By mid-year, students should be accurately decoding a few phonetically regular, one-syllable words with the c-v-c (*bat, run*) and v-c-e (*cake, late*) patterns. They should be able to read pseudo-words such as *dit, buf,* and *yode* (Bryant, 1975), and they should begin using this knowledge to sound out unknown words when reading text. Students should begin to use some regular c-v-c and v-c-e patterns in their invented spelling, though one might expect that reading these patterns would be easier than writing them, and should, therefore, come a little before the correct spelling of the patterns (Gentry, 2000a).

By the end of first grade, students should have accumulated over 100 words that they can recognize automatically. Their word-specific knowledge includes detailed information, such as being able to read and understand *to, too,* and *two,* and knowing that *green* is spelled g-r-e-e-n and not g-r-e-n-e. They should recognize many common irregularly spelled words such as *have, said,* and *where* and they should spell many first-grade level spelling words, such as *the, at, bed, cut,* and *five* correctly (Gentry, 2000a). This tremendous growth in underlying knowledge sources for reading and spelling enables students, by the end of first grade, to master the alphabetic system. They become consolidated alphabetic readers who have advanced to Stage 4.

STAGE 4—CONSOLIDATED ALPHABETIC

Stage 4 students are able to use the alphabetic system in virtually the same way that you and I use it as adults. By now, they are able to read easy chapter books such as *Amelia Bedelia* by Peggy Parish and *Frog and Toad*

Are Friends by Arnold Lobel. They can navigate elaborate stories that extend over several pages and have unfamiliar and varied vocabulary, complex sentence structures, and few pictures to cue specific words in the text.

Their spelling knowledge has been consolidated as well. By now they use virtually the same system to spell as adult literate spellers, albeit with a relatively small stock of perfect spellings. A great deal of word-specific knowledge is yet to be developed. Nonetheless, they spell more than half the words they use in their writing correctly by the end of first grade and use easily recognized visual spelling patterns in the spellings they invent.

Figure 2.2 shows the way four of Ehri's phases of decoding (Ehri, 1997; Ehri and Wilce, 1985) dovetail with Gentry's stages of invented spelling (Gentry, 1982; 2000b) as well as when one might expect these stages to occur when students are developmentally on track.

ASSESSING CHILDREN IN THE INITIAL PHASES/STAGES OF READING AND DEVELOPMENTAL SPELLING

Ehri's Phases of Word Learning	Gentry's Stages of Spelling	
1. Pre-alphabet	Stage I: Pre-communicative	Mid-K
2. Partial Alphabetic	Stage II: Semi-phonetic	End of K
3. Full-Alphabetic	Stage III: Phonetic	Mid First
4. Consolidated Alphabetic	Stage IV: Transitional	End of First
Reading Phases	**Spelling Stages**	

Figure 2.2

MIKE SMITH—THE JOURNEY BEFORE FOURTH-GRADE LEVEL

Let's zoom in on one of your fourth-, fifth-, or sixth-grade readers whose development progressed normally. For our hypothetical student, Mike Smith, the stages of decoding development were clearly in sync with stages of invented spelling development. Mike Smith will give you a good sense of what is expected in literacy development under minimal literacy competency standards. You will get a good feel for the type of instruction that matches best to each stage of development. This exercise should give you insights into the type and timing of instruction for children in grades four, five, and six who function at these earlier levels of development.

MIKE SMITH—STAGE 1—FIRST HALF OF KINDERGARTEN

Mike was approximating reading and writing from the very first day of kindergarten. Soon he could read a few easy books from memory. As a Stage 1 pre-alphabetic reader and a Stage 1 semiphonetic speller, he did not use knowledge of sounds and letters to read unknown words when decoding, nor did he use knowledge of sounds and letters to invent spellings. He knew very little about how the alphabetic system represents speech. He read environmental print like *McDonald's* by remembering cues, such as its golden arches, but did not use any letters in the word's spelling (Masonheimer, Drum, and Ehri, 1984). He could read and write *7-Up,* using some arbitrary association with the marks on the label. He probably did not recognize 7 as a numeral, or /u/sound for *u,* or final consonant /p/ for *p.* Even though he could read *up* in *7-Up,* he could neither read *cup* nor *pup* if he saw them in print.

Mike Smith might have written a grocery list that looked like the one in Figure 2.3.

Figure 2.3

If you asked him to read the list he could approximate reading by telling you what he intended it to say:

"This says 7-Up." (Mike points to *7-Up.*)
"Branflakes." (Mike points to EOOS.)
"Milk." (Mike points to FISOS.)
"And donuts." (Mike points to MSOOE.)

Mike's Stage 1 reading dovetails with his Stage 1 spelling: both pre-alphabetic stages are characterized by little or no ability to use the alphabetic system. As a Stage 1 speller, Mike used letters in his approximations, but he did not know that letters represent sounds. Figure 2.4 shows teaching guidelines for Stage 1 decoders and spellers:

TEACHING GUIDELINES FOR STAGE 1 DECODERS AND SPELLERS

- Read aloud and have book talks.
- Introduce beginner-oriented texts and model reading them.
- Conduct shared and interactive reading sessions using beginner-oriented texts.
- Encourage independent reading. Match students with books they can read independently, using memorization or picture cues. Include a lot of easy books that have three to five words per page and a clear picture to print match along with predictable text (book levels 1-2; A-B). Include wordless picture books, easy alphabet or letter books, caption books, easy decodable books, keep books (Fountas and Pinnell, 1996), and homemade books (short, simple text dictated by the child using language experience approach).
- Model and help students develop an awareness of sounds in words.
- Have students sort picture cards based on sounds.
- Teach the letters of the alphabet.
- Have students match pictures with labels by beginning letters.
- Model writing.
- Model use of letters' sounds when writing (sound spelling).
- Use language experience approach.
- Introduce independent writing. Have students draw a picture and write about it. Accept any level (scribbling, using magic lines) as a starting point (Feldgus and Cardonick, 1999).
- Guide students in phonics-based spelling (Feldgus and Cardonick, 1999).
- Introduce underwriting, where adult writes conventionally below child's text (Feldgus and Cardonick, 1999).
- Introduce dialogue journals as students become more independent writers (Feldgus and Cardonick, 1999).
- Keep track of the student's spelling development.
- Model Stage 2 spelling. Move students beyond Stage 1 random letter spelling by modeling prominent sound/letter matches.

Figure 2.4

Mike's move from Stage 1 to Stage 2, which happened by the end of kindergarten, is a move from non-use to partial use of the alphabetic system in both decoding words and inventing spellings. In spelling, he advanced from using random letters at Stage 1 to partial or abbreviated spellings at Stage 2—from FISOS to MK for *milk*. When decoding unknown words, he advanced from not using letter-sound correspondences to recognizing and using some prominent letter/sound correspondences, although he used only a partial cueing system for letter/sound representation.

At Stage 2, Mike often confused words that were visually similar—*big* for *bag* or *stop* for *Spot*. His miscues changed from Stage 1 to Stage 2 as illustrated in the following vignette:

In kindergarten, students at Stages 1 and 2 are introduced to easy-to-read books. They learn to read them from memory. The books usually have three to five words on a page and a clear picture to print match. These books contain high-frequency words and present concepts familiar to kindergartners. The language in the books approximates the kindergartner's spoken and aural language. These books often have a repetitive, predictable sentence stem.

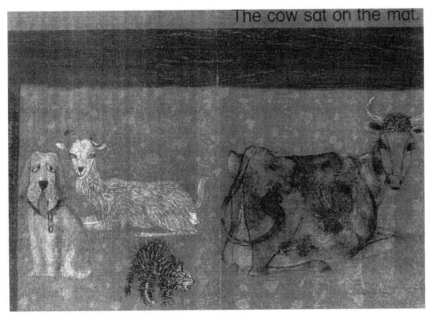

Figure 2.5

Figure 2.5 is a page from an easy book, *Cat on the Mat* by Brian Wildsmith, that might be found in Mike Smith's kindergarten book bag. When this book is introduced and the reading modeled by the teacher, Mike can soon join in the reading. Sometimes, after the pattern is established for Mike, he can read it on his own.

The title page shows a large tabby cat on a mat. Mike reads, "Cat on the Mat."

Pages 2-3 show the cat repositioned on the large red mat. Mike reads, "The cat sat on the mat."

Pages 4-5 show a dog joining the cat at the other end of the mat. Mike reads, "The dog sat on the mat."

Pages 6-7 show a goat joining the cat and the dog. Mike reads, "The goat sat on the mat."

On pages 8-9, shown in Figure 2.5, Mike encounters an unknown word—*cow*. Here's where it gets interesting. If he's a Stage 1 reader who grew up on a farm and developed an amazing knowledge of farm animals, his miscue on cow may be very different at Stage 1 than at Stage 2.

Instead of reading "A *cow* sat on the mat," a Stage 1 kindergartner once read this to me as "A *heifer* sat on the mat." I pointed to the word *cow* and asked why he thought it said *heifer*. He looked at me in astonishment and explained the arbitrary cues he had used to figure out the word:

"Look, it's a young cow," he said pointing to the picture. "It has a big sack," he continued, "and it's fat so I can tell it hasn't had its calf yet!"

At Stage 2, assuming Mike Smith knew the letter *c*, he might focus on a prominent letter in *cow* when decoding the unknown word. Instead of guessing the word as *heifer*, he's much more likely to read *cow* as *cat* based on the *c*, because *cat* and *cow* are visually similar. Mike is putting his growing knowledge of how the alphabetic system works to use. He's also demonstrating growth in his use of the underlying knowledge sources for reading and spelling.

MIKE SMITH—STAGE 2—SECOND HALF OF KINDERGARTEN

As a Stage 2 semi-phonetic speller, Mike began to spell words using abbreviated spellings with some appropriate sound/letter correspondences such as MY MT BT for "my motor boat." He also memorized the spellings of a few words perfectly. Figure 2.6 presents teaching guidelines for Stage 2 decoders and spellers.

For specific information on working with Stage 1 and Stage 2 readers and spellers to teach writing and the alphabetic system, I recommend *Kid Writing: A Systematic Approach to Phonics, Journals, and Writing Workshop* by Eileen G. Feldgus and Isabell Cardonick (The Wright Group, 1999).

TEACHING GUIDELINES FOR STAGE 2 DECODERS AND SPELLERS

- Read aloud and have book talks.
- Introduce more advanced beginner-oriented books and model reading them.
- Conduct shared and interactive reading sessions using beginner-oriented texts.
- Encourage independent reading. Match students with books they can read independently, using memorization or picture cues. Include books similar to those introduced at Stage 1, but move to the next levels of text (book levels 2-3; B-C). Continue to include easy alphabet or letter books, caption books, decodable books, and homemade books (short, simple text dictated by the child using language experience approach, but with more text than at Stage 1).
- Model and help students develop an awareness of prominent sounds in words, expanding on sounds already learned.
- Have students sort picture cards based on sounds.
- Teach the letters of the alphabet that have not yet been mastered.
- Make sure students are beginning to have full command of the letters of the alphabet: recognizing, naming, writing, and matching letters to an appropriate sound.
- Work with onsets and rimes. (An *onset* is the letter or letters before the vowel of a syllable, such as /h/ in *hat*, /sc/ in *scat*. A *rime* is a vowel and any following consonants of a syllable, such as *at* in *hat* and *scat*.)
- Use Elkonin boxes (Griffith and Olson, 1992; Elkonin, 1993).
- Introduce word families. Students at Stage 2 aren't likely to be reading or spelling by analogy. Start with a few easy, high-frequency word families and other easy chunking activities.
- Use letter tiles for word building. Model and practice with students.
- Have students match pictures with labels by using beginning letters
- Model writing at a level appropriate for Stage 2.
- Model use of letters' sounds when writing (sound spelling).
- Continue to use the language experience approach to generate stories. Increase story length and sophistication.
- Encourage independent writing. Have students draw a picture and write about it, using dialogue journal format. (Feldgus and Cardonick, 1999).
- Continue to guide students in phonics-based spelling, expanding their knowledge of sound/letter correspondences (Feldgus and Cardonick, 1999).

- Continue underwriting (adult, conventional spelling), noting what students have done in their sound-spelling attempts. Use underwriting as a springboard for instruction (Feldgus and Cardonick, 1999).
- Keep track of the student's spelling development.
- Model Stage 3 spelling. Move students beyond Stage 2 abbreviated spelling by modeling more elaborate sound-spellings, including letter/sound matches for all the sounds in the word being spelled. This often will require special focus on medial sounds. For example, if the student writes MK for *milk*, model the sound spelling MELK; if he or she writes BT for *boat*, model the sound spelling BOT.

Figure 2.6

MIKE SMITH—STAGE 3—FIRST HALF OF FIRST GRADE

Mike entered first grade reading a few easy books from memory and recognizing some words by sight. He knew the letters of the alphabet, was beginning to demonstrate phonemic awareness, and was able to match appropriate letters to a few prominent sounds in words.

In the first half of first grade, he developed the underlying knowledge sources to make the following dramatic changes by the middle of first grade. He moved from using prominent letters to figure out unknown words to full alphabet reading, decoding more efficiently using letter-by-letter sequential decoding and more efficient word recognition. He began to read and spell by analogy, greatly increasing his use of chunking. He used his growing knowledge of phonics and greatly increased the number of words he recognized. Not only could he read *net*, he could also read *jet, bet, wet, let, get, set, fret,* and so on. He relied on the alphabetic nature of English to figure out words and moved from using prominent letters to decode to using sequential letter-by-letter decoding. He progressed three or four levels in reading, moving from books such as *Brown Bear, Brown Bear, What Do You See?* by Bill Martin (level C; 3) to *The Foot Book* by Dr. Seuss (level E; 5), *Zoo-looking* by Mem Fox (level G; 12), and *Goodnight Moon* by Margaret Wise Brown (level H; 8).

Mike's progress in spelling also reflected the move to the full alphabetic phase. By midyear in first grade, he was a Stage 3 phonetic speller; he could spell virtually all the sounds he heard in words. For the first time he could write anything he could say and it was phonetically readable. His writing also incorporated many known spellings. The Stage 3 phonetic spelling typical of Mike's level of development might have looked something like the sample in Figure 2.7.

The three Pig's Lillte
one bay a Muthr
PiG SeNt.
her three Lillte
PiG'S Ot iNot
The WoD'S
The Frst Litl PiG
Met a MaN With
a BuN Dl UV
CtRo The PiG seD
tA te MaN GiV ME
CtoR to BiLD My huose

Figure 2.7

Figure 2.8 presents teaching guidelines for Stage 3 decoders and spellers.

TEACHING GUIDELINES FOR STAGE 3 DECODERS AND SPELLERS

- Read aloud and have book talks.
- Introduce more advanced beginning- to middle-level first-grade texts. Move to greater variety and variability in texts. Avoid using only decodable text.
- Encourage independent reading. Match students with books they can read with about 95% word recognition accuracy (book levels 3-8; C-H).
- Teach phonics. Focus on about 45 letter/sound correspondences that have a utility rate high enough to justify instruction. (See Gentry, 2000, pp.79-87).
- Include decodable books in the instructional mix. Once patterns are introduced, use decodable texts that match the patterns being studied. (Mesmer, 1999).
- Avoid books with such a high level of decodability that the text doesn't make sense (Nan can fan Dan. Dan is in a can.).
- Teach sight words using techniques such as word walls (Gentry, 2000; Cunningham, 1995).
- Demonstrate chunking of spelling patterns, such as onsets and rimes and regular phonic patterns.
- Work with word families. Students at Stage 3 should begin to read by analogy. Focus on high-frequency word families and other easy chunking activities.

- Use letter tiles for word building. Model and practice with students.
- Do word sorts that match spelling patterns.
- Make flipbooks for word families.
- Model writing at a level appropriate for Stage 3.
- Move to focused attention on medial vowels.
- Encourage independent writing.
- Model conventions for basic capitalization and punctuation.
- Make use of dialogue journals (Feldgus and Cardonick, 1999).
- Keep track of the student's spelling development.
- Model Stage 4 spelling. Model spelling all the sounds in words. Show how to use chunks of spelling and phonics patterns.

Figure 2.8

MIKE SMITH—STAGE 4—END OF FIRST GRADE

By the end of first grade, Mike Smith used the same process for reading that you and I use as adults. He had reached Stage 4, Ehri's consolidated alphabet phase of decoding and Gentry's transitional stage of spelling. By now he could read comic books and easy-to-read chapter books. Comic books present a clear picture to print match and he *liked* to read them. His reading had moved from the full alphabetic stage in the middle of first grade to a more consolidated process with all the basic systems of reading intact. He had a good reserve of word-specific knowledge and could recognize more than 100 words automatically on sight. His reading was no longer word-bound. The "self-teaching" phenomenon kicked into high gear. The more Mike read, the more words he learned to read. His teacher's need to teach him sight words directly was, to some extent, supplanted by a need to increase his volume of reading. What Mike Smith needed now was a spark to ignite a fire of interest and time spent reading—to ignite a reading blaze that would keep burning!

Too often, the spark is snuffed out in the classroom. I believe lighting the spark may be even more important for fourth-, fifth-, and sixth-grade teachers than teaching comprehension. It's certainly more important than teaching the state capitals, a list of explorers, or a science concept. Reading is a vehicle for thinking and for gaining knowledge. How many scientists do you know who can't read?

One of the best examples I can share about the way to light the spark came from a parent I met while sitting in an airplane writing this chapter. Carol Hagan and I started talking about the way children develop literacy. She told me the following story about her son, Joe.

Joe had barely learned to read in first grade and experienced very limited success in second and third grade. His parents actually thought he had academic limitations. "We were convinced Joe was just going to be a very, very average student," Carol told me. They were wrong. The summer after Joe finished third grade, his family planned to go camping for a week. Being a good mom, Carol planned for activities to occupy Joe, "In case it rained," she told me. She bought Joe a stack of *Konan, the Barbarian* comic books. Almost twenty years later, she still remembers *Konan, the Barbarian* was the spark that lit Joe's fire! "We had read to him," she told me, "but before *Konan*, we couldn't get Joe to read. He never seemed interested in reading in school. That whole week, I remember seeing him immersed in the stack of comic books. Eventually, he owned every *Konan, the Barbarian* comic book ever published."

On that vacation, Joe became a reader—but that's not the end of Joe's story. Carol came up with other plans to engage both of her children in literacy. "We didn't have a lot of money to buy a lot of expensive books at that time," she told me. "I used to go to the public library and check out the beautiful coffee table books for a couple of weeks—beautifully illustrated books about animals, foreign countries, architecture—whatever I thought my children might be interested in. I just put them out and Joe and his sister would look at them and read them if they wanted to." I thought this was an incredibly good idea to incorporate into fourth-, fifth-, and sixth-grade classrooms.

When I stepped off the plane I found a newsstand directly across from my arrival gate. There, prominently displayed with *Time, Vogue, Men's Fitness,* and *Newsweek,* was the current edition of *Worth*. It featured a dazzling cover story, "The King of Hot: How Venture Capitalist Steve Jurvetson Discovered the Power of Disruption" written by Joe Hagan, a successful writer whose literacy had been ignited by *Konan, the Barbarian*!

Children become readers at Stage 4. Our hypothetical student, Mike Smith, knew the fundamentals of phonics necessary for reading at Stage 4, which he reached by the end of first grade. Though he would increase his knowledge of how to use phonics, especially in polysyllabic words, and would continue to study phonics patterns in learning to spell words perfectly, he entered second grade with most of the phonics knowledge he needed for reading.

If you looked at Mike's Stage 4 spelling as he entered second grade it probably looked a lot like the sample in Figure 2.9.

Good THING to Eat
I Like STRALBARES and I like ORRANGE.
I like tomato SUPE and I like PECHIS.
I like apples and I like BROCULE.
I like COLEFALWORE TO, you know.
I like corn and I like green BENES.
I like FRIDE CHEKEN and I like BARBO Q CHEKEN.
But most of all I like HO MAED SPOGATE.
THOSS things are good for you.
That why I put them down.

Figure 2.9

Mike could already spell correctly about two thirds of the words he used in a piece of writing and could invent spellings for the rest of the words. Unfortunately, the misspelled invented spellings were often the words that seemed to preoccupy his teachers and parents. Not that they weren't important words, but Mike would need many years of word-specific study, including spelling study in grades four, five, and six, to gain the underlying word knowledge required for perfect spelling. Figure 2.10 presents teaching guidelines for Stage 4 decoders and spellers.

TEACHING GUIDELINES FOR STAGE 4 DECODERS AND SPELLERS

- Read aloud and have book talks.
- Introduce more advanced middle to end of first-grade level texts. Offer greater variety and variability in texts.
- Encourage independent reading. Match students with books they can read with about 95% word recognition accuracy (book levels 9-15; F-I).
- Teach basic phonics that is not yet mastered. Continue to focus on about 45 letter/sound correspondences that have a utility rate high enough to justify instruction. (Gentry, 2000, pp.79-87).
- Teach sight words using techniques such as word walls. Make sure the reader has a sight vocabulary of 100 high-frequency words. (Gentry, 2000; Cunningham, 1995).
- Demonstrate chunking of spelling patterns and regular phonic patterns both in reading and writing. Add to the student's repertoire of known patterns.
- Do word sorts that match spelling patterns.
- Model writing at a level appropriate for Stage 4.
- Encourage independent writing.
- Master conventions for basic capitalization and punctuation.

- Keep track of the student's spelling development.
- Model Stage 4 spelling. Model spelling all the sounds in words. Show how to use chunks of spelling and phonics patterns.
- Introduce spelling word lists of about six words per week. Focus on high-frequency words and patterns used in writing.

Figure 2.10

THE UNDERPREPARED—HOW TO GUIDE CHILDREN WHO HAVE NOT MET GRADE-LEVEL BENCHMARKS

What about those fourth, fifth, and sixth graders who write and spell like second graders? Or students with reading levels way below par? The solution is quite simple. You have to meet them where they are. You must put them on the grade-level map where they are functioning. In areas where they function like third graders, you must put them on a third-grade map, such as the one provided in *The Literacy Map: Guiding Children to Where They Need to Be (K-3)*. The map that fits each child will guide your instruction in individual conferences and in small groups. Intervention by a specialist will also guide the instruction when the problem is severe.

Here's an example of what I mean by matching students to the appropriate map. Fifth graders who spell on a second-grade level must be matched with second-grade level words and patterns. They must be working on benchmarks (see Figure 2.11) found in the second-grade literacy map.

SPELLING	Not Yet	Stage 4	Beyond Stage 4
2-21. Continues to spell many unknown words "by eye" (i.e., Stage 4, transitional spelling) while using specific word knowledge to spell an increasing number of second-grade-level words correctly			
2-22. Moves from inventing about one third of the spellings in pieces of independent writing to more accurate spelling	Not Yet	Some/Sometimes	All/Always
2-23. Begins to spell common structural patterns and inflectional endings correctly	Not Yet	Some/Sometimes	All/Always
2-24. Spells previously studied second grade level words and spelling patterns in his/her own writing			

Figure 2.11

These same students may be reading on a fifth-grade level; nevertheless, they will require spelling instruction that fits their particular needs.

It doesn't work to have a fifth grader who can't spell *nail, sleep, cash, horses,* and *wanted* memorize a fifth-grade list of 20 words, such as *modern, receive, through,* and *chocolate.* The development of word-specific knowledge at a sophisticated level must be built on lower-level, more basic, underlying knowledge.

MANAGING STUDENTS OF DIFFERING ABILITIES

If you teach fourth grade, the literacy map for grade four is not the only map you use. You will have to discover the maps that match each of the students in your classroom. Literacy maps help you know your students individually and guide them to literacy success.

Managing a class of students with a wide range of abilities is a challenge faced by every elementary school teacher. You may never encounter a classroom of students who come to you ready for grade-level instruction in each of the essential areas of literacy. Some will be reading, writing, or spelling below—maybe far below—grade level. A few may be reading, writing, or spelling far above grade level. Assessment and knowing each student individually are the keys to meeting the instructional challenge.

In the chapter that follows, you'll see the way a classroom schedule and management routine helps you turn a heterogeneous mass of individuals into a successful, working community of learners.

CHAPTER 3

SCHEDULES AND CLASSROOM MANAGEMENT

By Lynn Pott and Tony Stead

Most schools already have an overcrowded curriculum. More than likely, you must teach reading, writing, spelling, vocabulary, math, social studies, science, and history. You may even be asked to teach visual and performing arts, technology, values and citizenship, languages, health, and physical education. How can you do it all and do it effectively? One way is to put literacy first: without your effective literacy instruction, none of the other learning is possible.

Establishing a daily literacy block can help you juggle your many responsibilities sensibly. The literacy block is the time in each school day when you enhance each child's opportunity for literacy learning by directly teaching reading, writing, spelling, and vocabulary. This chapter will enable you to reassess your priorities and restructure your schedule. You may find confirmation for what you are already doing or you may decide to refocus your attention. I hope the chapter will help clarify the mission of elementary schooling—a mission that must be reflected in the schedule.

Last year, I visited a beautiful science magnet school in Florida. This stunning facility even had its own planetarium! Children came from a mixed but largely middle- class community. The people I met took pride in the school and the faculty was diligent. The day I visited, staff members from Busch Gardens Tampa Bay presented an engaging, hands-on educational program with exotic live animals. It was a wonderful event, but not uncommon in this school. Yet in spite of all these resources—hard-working teachers and obvious intellectual stimulation for students—there was a problem. The school was failing in the teaching of literacy. No one seemed to understand why a school with so many resources and so much effort did so poorly on the state's standards test. The school had received a C on the governor's rating scale, and, in this community, with those resources, C meant failure. Why did this school fail? I suspect I know the answer: the educators did not sufficiently know students individually as readers, writers, and spellers. The focus on literacy and literacy benchmarks for each child was missing.

The school's administrators talked to me about their mission to create a school ecology built around science to nurture scientific thinkers. Unable to get beyond the discussion of the C rating, I bit my tongue and held back from saying what was on my mind: "But do you understand what's supposed to happen in elementary school? There's not a scientist in America who can't read!"

A science magnet school is a wonderful idea. But all elementary schools, including special schools like this one, must have reading/writing classrooms in which literacy benchmarks get first priority. Reading, writing, spelling, and math is what elementary school is all about. If that fact is not reflected in your school's mission and in your own classroom schedule, you may need to reassess your curriculum.

In many schools, fourth-, fifth-, and sixth-grade teachers may need to transform the ecology of schooling so students will meet literacy benchmarks. This transformation requires a two to two-and-one-half hour literacy block every day to monitor and assess each student's literacy development and to allow enough time for teaching literacy. All other aspects of elementary education—science, health, history, and citizenship—may, in part be integrated into this block as children read, discuss, write, and respond using literacy. This is the time when the teacher finds out as much as possible about each student as a reader, writer, and speller, and establishes starting points for instruction. The teacher uses this information to drive classroom instruction (Hill and Crevola, 1999. "Chapter 6: The Role of Standards in Educational Reform for the 21st Century" p.127). Finding out as much as possible about each student (knowing each student individually as a reader, a writer, and a speller) enables the teacher to teach each student based on his or her position on the literacy map.

Both research and practice have established the need for classroom literacy programs in grades four, five, and six that consist of reading, writing, and spelling workshops conducted within a teaching block of at least two hours per day (Hill and Crevola, 1999). Because the student's growth as a reader and as a writer are inextricably connected, separating these processes is inefficient. Both processes share the same underlying knowledge sources. The processes are reciprocal. Researchers often describe reading and writing as mutually dependent collaborative activities (Dyson, 1989; Ehri, 1984; Hansen, 1987; Hansen, Newkirk, and Graves, 1985; Hynes, 2000). Author Toni Morrison writes eloquently on the reading/writing connection from the perspective of the writer:

Writing and reading are not all that distinct for a writer. Both exercises require being alert and ready for unaccountable beauty, for the intricateness or simple elegance of the writer's imagination, for the world that imagination evokes. Both require being mindful of the places where imagination sabotages itself, locks its own gates, pollutes its vision. Writing and reading mean being aware of the writer's notions of risk and safety, the serene achievement of, or sweaty fight for, meaning and response-ability.

(Morrison, 1992)

In planning this chapter, I invited two educators to make contributions based on their experiences with schedules in fourth-, fifth-, and sixth-grade classrooms. The first was Lynn Pott. I visited over 100 elementary schools last year. None impressed me more than Henry Elementary School near St. Louis, where Dr. Lynn Pott is principal. She gave me a tour, showed me children's work, introduced me to her staff, described what was going on in their school community and I thought, "Why aren't more elementary schools like this?" Getting to know principals like Lynn is one of the joys of my work. Based on my overwhelmingly positive impression of Lynn and her school, I asked her to contribute to this book, but I gave her a tough assignment: " Lynn, your school just feels right! Based on what you have experienced and what's happening here, help me and others understand scheduling." On page 36 you will find guidelines for creating a schedule, on which Lynn and I collaborated. These guidelines will help you think about your own schedule.

The second contribution is by master teacher Tony Stead. I have attended Tony's workshops and admired Tony's work for years. Tony taught elementary school in Australia for 14 years and lectured at the University of Melbourne before coming to America where he currently works as an educational consultant. Having taught fourth and fifth grade, Tony brings practical knowledge to a discussion of the way to manage a fourth-, fifth-, and sixth-grade schedule.

A number of scheduling possibilities can work for grades four, five, and six. Each school setting provides a unique set of scheduling strengths and challenges. Guidelines for creating a schedule provided by Lynn and Tony's sample schedule will help you begin to evaluate your own schedule to determine whether it places an appropriate focus on literacy. Lynn's sample schedules may be found in the appendix. Before reviewing Lynn's guidelines and Tony's schedule, take time to think about their insights.

THE SCHEDULING DILEMMA—SEEING COMPLETELY
By Lynn Pott

Every teacher has experienced frustration associated with scheduling. Changing your schedule may not be a matter of "seeing wrong" but a matter of "seeing completely." A discussion of the way to create appropriate classroom schedules in grades four, five, and six begins with a commitment to the importance of teaching literacy. It gives precedence to developing children as thinkers, readers, writers, and word users. The discussion begins with the realization that you need two to two-and-one-half hours each day in grades four, five, and six to teach literacy. As principal of an elementary school, I realize how difficult it can be to establish a consistent, daily, two to two-and-one-half hour literacy block. Pullouts for reading, special education services, orchestra, and many other conflicts can jeopardize that critical block of time.

Restructuring your schedule begins with a mindset that reflects a dedication for knowing your students as individuals—as readers, writers, spellers, and thinkers. It begins with awareness that you are not only a teacher, but also a literacy observer, a literacy researcher, a sponsor of reading and writing, and a literacy learning advocate for each child. I believe your most important job as an elementary teacher is teaching literacy. Your mindset must embrace the fact that teaching and engaging in literacy require time and a consistent and predictable environment.

The classroom should be a place where the child thinks a lot and uses literacy to express his or her ideas. I don't believe one can teach literacy without some understanding of each child's interests, passions, and anxieties as well as a lot of opportunities for the child to express them. Teachers must see and understand what each student is doing in reading and writing before they know which strategies or skills to teach. Only then can the teacher assess what each student needs and decide what to do next.

A scheduled time for reading and writing allows for ongoing assessment, conferencing, and opportunities to work with individuals and small groups. It allows students to compare, contrast, think about, and learn from their own writing in the context of their classmates' writing, the writing modeled by teachers, and the writing by authors the students are reading. Children begin to see themselves as a community of writers, a family of readers, or, as Frank Smith puts it, a literacy club in which literacy becomes a part of the child's everyday life (Smith, 1988).

Time is a key factor for literacy. Researchers report high correlation between the amount of time students read and reading achievement beyond the early grades (Anderson, Hiebert, Scott, and Wilkinson, 1985; Adams, 1990). Empirical research has not yet clarified how specific practices such as independent silent reading are causally related to increased reading skill (Report of the National Reading Panel, 2000). Nevertheless, it is clear that fourth, fifth and sixth graders who do not read and write do not make progress in these areas or develop their full potential as thinkers.

I had to rethink my own schedule years ago when I taught fifth grade. My own learning evolved as I watched the dramatic change in one of my students that occurred after I established a predictable schedule for reading and writing. Before the schedule change, Yvonne (not her real name) did not want to write or read, and she was angry part of each day. She and I did not seem to connect. Yvonne wasn't making much progress, and my failure to connect with her was a total mystery. I now find it quite remarkable that much of what was going wrong was directly related to my classroom schedule.

When Yvonne first entered my classroom, the language arts schedule was "hit or miss." We might write one day, but the next day we would do something else. As Donald Graves has explained, writing taught once or twice a week is just frequent enough to remind students that they can't write (Graves, 1994). My schedule had no established routines for Yvonne. The students could not set priorities and I had not set priorities for how we should be spending our time.

Yvonne had not been functioning well in a schedule that seemed to focus primarily on "doing things"—often in isolated activities, centers, or projects. Of course, the things we were doing seemed to be important, but as I look back, they were without the appropriate purpose or specific literacy goals. Although we had reading lessons every day, I rarely conferenced with individual students or conducted mini-lessons based on individual needs. I did very little personal assessment of individual learners. In fact, I really didn't know my students as individual learners. I relied entirely on a basal program, standardized tests, curriculum guides, and workbooks to determine which skills to teach. I was managing my classroom as if the students were dispensable blue-collar workers in an auto parts factory. If they didn't fit into the regimen and get work completed on time, they didn't make the grade.

Workbooks and canned tests were not giving me a true picture of how students like Yvonne were functioning. While some of the basals and tests may have been good resources, I had allowed them to drive the curriculum rather than steer it myself or put my students in the driver's seat. At that time, I really didn't know Yvonne as a reader, a writer, a thinker, or a human being. I knew her as a student who was either turning in a workbook assignment or who was disrupting the class and not getting her work done. At the same time, I found myself experiencing a great deal of frustration.

The year I taught Yvonne was the year I enrolled in a post-graduate degree program at Columbia University. My classes with Mary Ellen Giacobbe, Nancie Atwell, and Lucy Calkins prompted me to rethink my classroom schedule and what I had been doing. I began to understand how my inconsistent, unpredictable classroom environment was working against Yvonne and the other students as readers and writers. At this same time a powerful book, *Lessons From a Child* by Lucy Calkins, prompted me to see Yvonne and students like her more completely. A schedule change—gradual at first and starting with the implementation of a writing workshop—reshaped my classroom, my philosophy, and my teaching.

My total perception of Yvonne was an epiphany. I came to realize that my frustration with Yvonne was rooted, to a large extent, in scheduling practices that didn't work. Yvonne refused to read and write. She frequently became angry and yelled in class. Her anger resulted in disruptions for other students. I dreaded these encounters, but I had never asked, "Why did they happen?"

In the second month of school, I found myself reevaluating my program schedule. I switched to a writing workshop on a consistent, systematic basis. I established routines in a 60-minute writing block each day. This schedule change allowed me to begin to look closely at what individual students were doing, what they knew already, and what they needed to learn. I began to ask "Why?" more and I began to get answers. I also noticed remarkable changes in students, especially Yvonne.

The young girl who was angry, agitated, and disruptive was finding comfort and solace in a smoother, predictable classroom routine in which she found me treating her as an important and dignified individual learner. She was no longer just some respondent to a workbook sheet or a "performer" in a reading group like a factory worker who had to reach a quota—so many words spelled correctly on a test or so many pages in a workbook marked correctly. Yvonne was finding new avenues for expressing herself and she was finding that people actually cared about what she had to say. During our newly formed writing workshop, angry outbursts began to subside. Yelling was replaced with discussions. I marveled as Yvonne began to communicate with her peers. She solicited classmates' ideas, often sharing her own and listening intently to theirs. After two months of daily writing workshop, Yvonne took her seat in the Author's Chair to share a piece of her writing. Sitting confidently in front of the 26 members of her "language arts family" she shared a poem. Her classmates' attention was rapt, as all eyes—eyes that communicated deep admiration and respect—were on Yvonne.

Daddy
Why did he have to die?
Boy, do I miss him a lot!
He meant everything to me.
Now, he's only in my heart.

As I listened to Yvonne share her poem I saw a transformation not only in this child, but in our classroom—in the way we viewed our work together and in the way we viewed each other. As children responded to the poem we learned the seed of Yvonne's anger. She had seen her father stabbed. Right there in language arts, Yvonne unveiled the hurt she was enduring because she no longer had a father. Instead of being intimidated by her anger, Yvonne's classmates responded with empathy and acceptance. A change in schedule, a change in how we responded to each other, a change to viewing literacy as an opportunity to express and learn about what was meaningful in our lives, had transformed our classroom community. We were seeing more completely. I was also connecting with Yvonne, not only personally, but also academically: I was better able to meet her needs as a reader, a writer, and a speller.

This poem was the tip of an iceberg. Children began asking Yvonne to expand her writing on this topic. There was also a larger story here. Students began sharing their own worries, feelings, and successes—willing to tread where they had not taken risks before.

In my struggle to make readers and writers of my students, I found myself being remade as a teacher. I began to feel a need to take more risks myself—especially with my schedule. At the same time, I was gaining confidence and respecting myself more as a teacher. My next step was to move from traditional reading groups to reading workshop with small guided reading groups, mini-lessons, conferencing, sharing, and a focus on knowing each student as a reader. The reading specialist came into the room to work with students with special needs. We started working together—team teaching the mini-lessons, conferencing with students, facilitating sharing times. The reading specialist provided excellent modeling of reading strategies and helped me to grow as a teacher. In my experience, it worked well to have the reading specialist work with students in my classroom rather than pull them out. Working within the classroom brought consistency in routines, goals, expectations, and terminology and strategies the students were learning for literacy development. This team teaching worked especially well because the reading teacher provided special training that I did not have. I learned new strategies for teaching literacy and improved my own professional effectiveness by watching her interact with students. It was a collaborative learning experience for both of us.

A great deal had changed beyond my schedule: I looked at the classroom as 26 individuals rather than three reading groups. I understood the purpose of truly knowing each child individually. Because writing, reading, and responding were all windows into their minds, I not only began to see each child more completely, but was able to use what I was learning about each child to meet his or her needs. The change in schedule was the catalyst. The reading and writing workshops, without interruptions and with appropriate time and attention to insure each child's development, were bringing out the "real reader and writer" in each one of them. Each and every child was becoming a writer and a reader engaged in both processes. It was personal and social. It regenerated itself.

THE CARE TEAM

Understanding the importance of knowing and caring for each student individually is now school-wide policy in my elementary school. An example of how we work together to meet each student's individual needs is our school-wide Care Team. Each Thursday, we conduct a Care Team meeting before school. It is led by counselors and includes building administrators, a special education teacher, reading specialists, school nurse, physical education teachers, a music teacher, and an art teacher. A classroom teacher schedules a time to discuss a particular student who may need special attention. At that meeting strategies are brainstormed and interventions are discussed to help make the child successful.

The referral to Care Team requires the teacher to know the student as a reader, writer, and speller. Samples of writing, analysis of skills, documentation from one-on-one conferences are sent to each team member prior to the meeting. This helps the entire group know the child's level of achievement. That knowledge allows the session to be devoted to the discussion of strategies and interventions and educational issues instead of rehashing discipline problems. I see a direct link between scheduling changes that allow teachers to know students individually and successful interventions, such as the Care Team.

BLOCK SCHEDULES

Research supports that scheduling language arts in big blocks of time works (Hill and Crevola, 1999). Readers and writers require time for concentration. Teachers require time to nurture readers and writers: time for modeling, time for holding the students' hands as they try out what the teacher has modeled, and time for students to practice, in a meaningful context, what was modeled.

In addition, I believe students also require routines just as real writers do. Writers usually write at a certain time, often in a specific place, and frequently even with specific pens. Routines, a boon to classroom management, help students settle down and get to work.

Another epiphany was that reading and writing have to be intertwined. A student who will develop his or her full potential as a writer must be a reader. Children must read voraciously to prepare for writing. Reading spurs the child's thoughts, provides new knowledge, models new ways of presenting information, and shows the way other writers use words or phrases.

As a teacher you must find the time for reading and writing workshop. Since reading and writing are tangible forms of the thinking process, these workshops produce tremendous gains in other subject areas as well. Students' independent reading and writing flow naturally in and out of all subject areas. The teacher must take enough time with the reading and writing to model, raise expectations, match students with appropriate texts, and direct students into new content areas of learning. The teacher also must allow each student to take control by becoming a reader and a writer, rather than someone who merely hands in assignments (Graves, 1983). Ultimately, the student must sit in the driver's seat. (See Chapter 5 for an example of how Sarah and Kaisa, guided by a master teacher, take control of their own writing development in grades four, five and six.)

Recognize that, you must schedule two to two-and-one-half hours of consistent, uninterrupted time for reading, writing, and spelling. Reading, writing, and spelling (and math) are the tools of language that students use to think and gain knowledge in other areas. Students need to know that they will have regular chunks of time not only for writing and reading, but also for anticipating and planning for these events. A consistent literacy block and routine will develop the writer's mindset in each student so that each one knows what to expect and how to plan for it. In the words of Nancie Atwell, students "need time to write well" (Atwell, 1987).

One of my fifth-grade students, Alice, developed the writer's mindset. She was in the grocery store with her mother and a younger sister. Even though her sister was being a nuisance, Alice's mother reprimanded Alice. Alice later told me that she was pretty upset about the situation, but she knew she could use the event as a topic for writing workshop. That might help her deal with her hurt feelings. "I grabbed a recipe card from the produce section and borrowed a pen from my mom," she told me. The notes taken in the grocery store became the seed for a biographical narrative:

There I was not even two, and they went out and got another one. Didn't they think I was good enough? My new sister—she was like a movable noise-making toy, but she was never put away!

Another fifth grader, Sheri, operating with the same writer's mindset, wrote the kernel for a piece of writing one evening when she was home alone with her brother. She heard a noise and ran into the bathroom to hide, and she captured her thoughts on a tissue. The next morning in our writing conference she shared the following:

I got scared. I heard a noise and ran to the bathroom. I know I shouldn't watch those movies!

Because Sheri knew that writing was a regular part of each day, she seized this opportunity to be prepared. The ideas for writing topics began to flow naturally into our writing workshop. Other students learned by watching their peers and more kernels for writing came into the classroom on tissues, napkins, scratch pads, and recipe cards.

But the classroom changes went far beyond sharing topics for writing. Building a community of learners for literacy, connecting with students individually, and finding out as much as possible about each student made it possible for me to do my own work more effectively. I found it easier to achieve my teaching objectives, such as matching individuals with books, engaging them as readers and writers, teaching word-specific knowledge, and modeling comprehension strategies.

The particulars of schedules can vary. What cannot vary is the regularity of the schedule, the ways in which teacher and student operate in the schedule, and how student and teacher spend their time. Here is a list of basic guidelines to help you create a schedule for language arts that works:

GUIDELINES FOR CREATING A SCHEDULE

1. Commit to the importance of teaching literacy. Make the changes needed in scheduling to reflect this commitment.
2. Commit to a specific time each day for reading, writing, and spelling.
3. Create a schedule that is consistent and predictable.
4. Allocate time. Implement a two-hour literacy block in grades four, five, and six.
5. Decide that your schedule must enable you to know each student individually as a reader, writer, speller, and thinker.
6. Create a schedule that increases the volume of reading, writing, spelling, and responding.

7. Set learning goals for each student based upon ongoing assessment that shows the student's current level of functioning and allows you to determine a literacy map to guide him or her to higher levels of reading, writing, and spelling.

8. Manage your classroom with easy-to-follow routines and procedures so students know what is expected on a daily and weekly basis.

9. Do not allow pullouts, external interruptions, during the literacy block. Make this a school-wide policy.

10. Use the literacy block for ongoing assessment. Allow assessment-performance-assessment cycle to inform your teaching.

BUILDING SCHEDULES AS A TEAM

Change is difficult. One of our teachers did not believe in the merit of the literacy block that included guided reading and writing workshops. Language lessons with daily worksheets were the norm in her classroom. Her method of structuring her teaching was not working well, yet, she was skeptical of the value of a consistent scheduled time for different blocks of literacy instruction. As a principal, I felt the responsibility to help bring about change. I realized I not only had to figure out how to secure more time for literacy, but also how to help teachers know how to use that time.

How did we start? Three years ago the grade level groups met with me for our first annual planning meeting to talk about the schedule, making literacy a priority, and review educational literature and research about scheduling. First, as a grade-level team, we discussed schedule changes and reviewed the literature. We held several meetings to discuss research articles that had been shared. Because I believe that an administrator should not get too far from the classroom, I went into the classroom of the reluctant teacher. I modeled a writing workshop, demonstrated ongoing assessment and record keeping, and furnished the teacher with mini-lessons. I did little things to try to help the teacher make the transition easier. For example, in order to provide an easy format for documentation, I gave her a binder with the students' names on tabs.

Equipped with more information and resources, my reluctant teacher began to change her focus to knowing her students individually and meeting their needs in reading and writing workshops instead of showering them with worksheets. Setting goals for scheduling, reviewing student-documented work, keeping records, and celebrating successes became part of a scheduled performance evaluation process. The transition was a yearlong process with additional support from our district language arts facilitator.

After four years, an appropriate literacy block is part of the schedule in every classroom in my school. This shift required establishing new mental models for teaching and scheduling. It required teachers to rely less on worksheets and to view themselves as professionals, to move from teaching a basal to teaching students to read and write, to move from giving tests and grading worksheets to becoming diagnosticians and experts in ongoing assessment. Teachers did not instantly accept ideas for schedule changes, but reading, writing, and spelling workshops are now a building-wide expectation.

Basic Steps in Securing Time for the Literacy Block
(Guided by the principal, facilitator, and grade-level team)

- Focus on the goal of literacy.
- Read, share, and discuss the research.
- Conduct grade-level discussions and planning meetings.
- Conduct individual discussions and planning meetings.
- Provide ongoing staff development.
- Provide model lessons in classrooms.
- Provide aides, such as record-keeping binders for teachers.
- Visit transition classrooms on a regular basis to celebrate successes.
- Focus on clearly stated goals for literacy and scheduling in performance evaluations.

MANAGING THE LITERACY BLOCK IN GRADES FOUR, FIVE, AND SIX
By Tony Stead

It was a cold Monday morning as the children in my split grade four/five entered the classroom. They looked exhausted from their weekend but were happy to be back in the classroom that they called their "second home." It took some time and planning to set up this environment, and it certainly broke with the tradition of what a fourth- and fifth-grade classroom should look like. For instance, the large library area full of books, soft toys, plants, and personal items children brought from home was not what you would expect to find in a "typical" upper-elementary classroom. Yet to me, they were essential to establish a warm environment that allowed children to feel comfortable in taking risks with their learning and becoming responsible learners. I remember the words of Sue, one of my fifth-grade learners when she asked, "Tony, can my mom come and see our room? It looks better than our house. She needs to see it to get some ideas."

The classroom library is the epicenter of the room: the heart, lungs, eyes, and ears of our daily routines during the literacy block. As I marveled at Sue's comment, I realized the room belonged to the children, not to me. Under my guidance, they became the ones who set up the schedule, decided who would take care of the plants, kept the room tidy, and had access to the space during independent reading or other special times when its use was specifically designated. They had come up with solutions for what would happen if someone mistreated the classroom library or misbehaved when they were using it. I had modeled to show them how to set up a schedule. Each week they voted on a classroom captain who helped organize the schedule for the week. Of course, they worked within clearly defined parameters. They knew, for instance, that our two-hour literacy block was divided into six segments, and they knew exactly what would happen each day in each segment and how long the activity would last. They knew that the classroom library was the meeting area where we held whole-class discussions, where I conducted reading and writing mini-lessons, and where I read aloud to students and conducted book talks. It was also where students took refuge when they needed a quiet place to read or to conference with each other.

One amazing outcome of our new structure was that the classroom was both organized and usually free from unacceptable behaviors. Without a structure in place to deal with negative behavior—and without the smooth movement of the students from one activity to the next—reading, writing, speaking, and word study become secondary to maintaining discipline and teachers usually lose focus. For me, setting up effective classroom management boiled down to four major issues:

1. Routines
2. Expectations
3. Responsibility
4. Consistency (clarity on what was expected and what would happen if those expectations were not met)

These issues formed the foundation of effective classroom management and spiraled through each segment of the literacy block.

The students were aware of what each of the six segments looked like and how long each would last. When possible, I think the literacy block should be scheduled first thing in the morning while students are fresh and eager to learn. Unfortunately, it doesn't always work out so smoothly—students may be scheduled for something special like art or library in the morning. When this happens, I simply begin my literacy block as early as possible and, if necessary, split the reading and writing components into two separate one-hour segments. Occasionally, a content-area segment gets left out on a particular day due to some special event.

The following literacy block schedule is displayed in the classroom library for all to see. Every student understands how each segment works and could explain what is supposed to happen.

SEGMENT I. Read Aloud and Book Talks or Shared Reading

Time: 15 minutes

Together we read and discuss literature. I read a book aloud and direct a book talk, or we do a shared reading in which everyone can see the same text.

In Segment I, students are aware that there are times when they can help me with the reading and times when I take responsibility for the reading. I explain that I do this to help them become better readers, to introduce new authors and genres, and to recommend different books they may select for their own independent reading. I allocate 15 minutes for Segment I and ask students to make sure I keep to the 15-minute limitation. Otherwise, they won't have enough time for independent reading, and I won't have enough time for small-group instruction.

The children like this routine because it gives them responsibility for keeping our schedule on track. I recall one occasion when the 15 minutes were up, as I was halfway through an exciting read aloud. James, one of my fourth graders, raised his hand and informed me that it was time to move to our next activity. However, he added that he was enjoying the story so much, he didn't mind if we went overtime! His classmates agreed and, even though I objected, I was out-voted and the read aloud continued. The class agreed that the following day we would restrict the read aloud to 10 minutes to make up for the time lost. I can still remember their faces: they were so excited and empowered to have some control about decisions made in the classroom. I often think that most discipline problems stem from students' feelings of disempowerment and lack of voice.

SEGMENT II. Guided Reading
     (two small groups, 20 minutes each)

     Literacy Activities and Independent Reading
     (for students who are not in the groups)

(NOTE: Students complete two different activities during this 40-minute block.)

Time: 40 minutes

I work with small groups of four to six students. I usually do guided reading or an instructional activity such as reciprocal teaching while the rest of the class is involved in literacy activities. The larger group may be doing independent reading out of their book bags, reading with buddies, selecting new books, listening to and reading a book on tape, or responding to literature via a number of response options. Once I've trained them, they may even be in "literacy clubs" or conducting their own small literature circles. In my classroom, everybody's reading!

Segment II is when most of the management nightmares come to life. Students who aren't in my reading group must be able to work independently, without me assisting them. I learned—through years of experience—to spend time establishing routines for what they should be doing before I "turn them loose." Depending on the students in the group and their previous experiences in working independently, getting students to function well in this schedule can be anywhere from easy to difficult. Eventually, even with the challenging groups, I got the schedule to run smoothly.

One observation I made over the years was that most management issues stemmed from students in the larger group failing to engage in appropriate reading materials. If I found students who were just pretending to read, I usually suspected they were not matched to an appropriate text.

A key to making things work is to organize the classroom library so that students can make appropriate selections easily. I put a lot of effort into guiding their selections. We talk about how to self-select appropriate books. These "just right books" are books students can read with about 95% word recognition accuracy. There is flexibility for choosing selections, including nonfiction titles, which aren't always read cover to cover. There is also flexibility that allows a student to choose a book that may be too hard in terms of word recognition. This works when the student is passionate about the topic and willing to put in the extra effort needed to get something out of the book.

I begin by asking students what helps them select a "just right book." Then we set up a "How to Choose Just Right Books" chart. I suggest some selection strategies and they add to the list. A sample might look like this:

HOW TO CHOOSE "JUST RIGHT BOOKS"

1. Look at the "blurb" on the cover to see if you can read and understand it.
2. Read a few passages to see if you can read and understand the text.
3. Ask someone in the classroom for recommendations.
4. Look at the color-coding of the book if it has one. (I color code the books in my classroom library according to reading level. The color-coding system helps students select "just right books.")
5. Make sure the book is about something that interests you.
6. Take time to browse through the book to make a good selection.

Then I raise the questions, "Are our books well organized? Would it be easier for you to find 'just right books' if we put the really hard books together, and the books that are not so hard together?" This usually makes sense to them, and physically organizing our books helps acquaint the students with the available selections. I have almost 1,000 books in my classroom collection. I usually end up with four or five baskets of books that go from easy to hard. The students color-code the books to make selecting and replacing books easy. (It is important to note all books are not organized by levels. I still have baskets of books organized by specific themes, interests, and authors.)

Another problem is the "book borrowing stampede." This occurs when students make their book selections, which may take up to 15 minutes. Too often they fight over books and make a lot of noise. To eliminate "book borrowing stampede," we set up a rotation that allows six children at a time to browse through the classroom library and make their selection for the week. We also set limits on the number of books they may borrow at a time.

At the beginning of the year, I don't jump into reading groups but spend time helping the six children in each rotation make appropriate choices. This allows me to get to know them better and do some ongoing assessment: "Elana, read this paragraph for me and let's see if this book is right for you" or "Did you consult the chart? What makes you think this is a 'just right book?'" Once I am confident they are able to select appropriate reading materials and are engaged in reading and comprehending the books they have selected, I start meeting small groups for guided reading or reciprocal teaching. A good indicator that independent reading is working—that they no longer need me to help them select books—is the first time they groan and complain when I tell them their 20 minutes of independent reading time is over. Students only complain if they are truly engaged in their reading and want it to continue.

In addition to independent reading, students' independent work revolves around literacy activities. Literacy activities are introduced one at a time with discussions of expectations and options. Here is a list of some possible independent literacy activities that keep children reading while I work with small groups.

TYPES OF 20-MINUTE LITERACY ACTIVITIES

Independent Reading
Buddy Reading
Reading Response
Reading at the Computer
Reading Books on Tape
Book Borrowing (selecting new books)
Literature Clubs

When students are engaged in talking and writing about literature in a small group, the room may get too noisy! I tackle the classroom noise problem by establishing "noise monitors." It is the role of these four children to remind groups to lower their voices if the discussion becomes too loud. Each child gets a turn at being a noise monitor for one week and wears a noise monitor tag to signify that status. The children know from discussions that the noise monitors have ultimate control and that if they do not adhere to the requests of the noise monitors, the consequences will be missing out on a favorite activity during the day.

I make sure that I first talk to the whole class about what is acceptable noise, and the ways noise monitors should politely respond to unacceptable noise from a group. As a result, instances of disturbance during small-group instruction become minimal. On one memorable occasion, Jorene, a noise monitor, interrupted my reading group. Noise monitors know full well that they should not interrupt my instruction unless it is an emergency. But Jorene couldn't help herself.

"Tony," she exclaimed, "I'm sorry, but the children are just so good. We should tell them they're good!" She was right. How easy it is to focus on the negative and not celebrate positive behavior. From that day on, noise monitors also had a new role: to congratulate groups who were on task.

Another way to control noise and to help students work well independently is to explain what is expected. For example, before the students begin responding to literature independently, we brainstorm and discuss several options for reading response. Our list ends up on a chart in the classroom library.

WAYS TO RESPOND TO LITERATURE

1. Write a book report.
2. Have a book talk with a friend.
3. Form a literature club.
4. Make up a sequel to the story you have just read.
5. Write a poem about the book.
6. Draw a diagram to show what happened in the book.
7. Write a response in your reading log.

A response in the reading log is always required for each book read. The other response is students' choice, and they could choose a different one each week. The completed response is checked off in their reading log under the title of the book. Having choices, routines, expectations, responsibilities, and clarity about what is expected contribute to responses to literature with few disruptions due to improper behavior.

Literature Circles, by Harvey Daniels and *Tell Me*, by Aidan Chambers are excellent resources that have helped me establish constructive and focused literature clubs in my classrooms. However, I spent months establishing routines for constructively talking about books before having students form literature clubs and use these techniques independently.

SEGMENT III. Sharing (Reading)

Time: 5 minutes

Students come together to share.

The third component of the block is a time for students to come together and share their learning. Each day, one student briefly talks about what he or she learned or recommends a good book to read. Children always know ahead of time who is sharing the following day so that they have time to prepare. Red stickers are placed on the sharing chart to keep track of who has shared and to ensure that each student gets a turn.

SEGMENT IV. Modeled or Shared Writing

Time: 20 minutes

This time is devoted to teaching writing to the whole group.

The fourth component of my literacy block is the beginning of our writing block. Students understand through discussion that this is a time for me to show them how to be better writers. There are times when we construct a piece together with me acting as the scribe. There are also times when I model for them what good writers do as they watch and listen. It's imperative that I have markers, chart paper, and an easel ready so that I don't waste time hunting for supplies, leaving students in the meeting area with nothing to do. I appoint supply monitors each week to take charge of this task, thus giving back responsibility for the smooth running of the literacy block.

I hold students responsible for helping me keep to the 20 minutes allocated for this schedule. Actually, they are better at sticking to the schedule than I am. They help me keep the literacy block in good focus and in balance.

SEGMENT V. Independent Writing

Time: 30 minutes

Students write independently. I work with small groups and with individuals.

The fifth component of my literacy block is one that takes time and patience to establish and maintain. This 30-minute time slot is when children engage in independent writing, which can be both teacher-directed and student-centered. Behavior and management can be problematic.

One of the big challenges is to make sure the students know what to do if they need assistance so they do not line up at my desk. It is also vital that I rove during this time, offering assistance and suggestions where necessary. To eliminate too many requests for assistance, I construct a "Helpers Chart." Each student writes his or her name and what they are good at. We learn to help each other. George, for example, wrote that he was a good speller. Children who couldn't find a word in the dictionary might go to George for help.

In addition to individual instruction, I often gather a small group of children for 10 to15 minutes for guided-writing instruction. These guided-writing groups are formed once the other students are able to work individually.

Noise monitors and supply monitors all are functioning during this time. A small cart loaded with supplies works well for publishing. At the end of the writing session, supply monitors make sure everything goes back in place. They report missing items to the class during whole-class discussion, and the class works together to solve any problems.

SEGMENT VI. Sharing (Writing)

Time: 10 minutes

Students share their work.

The final 10 minutes of the literacy block is a time for sharing. As with the reading share time, each student gets to share a piece of writing or something he or she has learned about being a writer. A yellow sticker designates when they have shared. All voices get equal opportunity to be heard.

By 11:00AM, students are lined up for gym. They are ready for a different kind of learning. We will add spelling/vocabulary building and additional oral language experiences to our schedule from 2:40–3:10, at the end of the day. A full day schedule is presented in Figure 3.1.

FULL DAY SCHEDULE
Fourth/Fifth Grade Combined

8:45-9:00	Morning Preparation
	Literacy Block 9:00-11:00
9:00-9:15	Segment I: Read Aloud and Book Talks or Shared Reading
9:15-9:35	Segment II: Guided Reading/Independent Reading and Literacy Activities
	Small-group instruction (teacher and one group)
	Independent reading and book borrowing (remainder of students)
9:35-9:55	Guided Reading (or Reciprocal Teaching)/Independent Reading and Literacy Activities
	Small-group instruction (teacher and one group)
	Literacy activities (remainder of group)
9:55-10:00	Segment III: Sharing (Reading) (whole class)
10:00-10:20	Segment IV: Modeled or Shared Writing (whole class)
10:20-10:50	Segment V: Independent Writing (whole class)
	(teacher roving or working with small group)
10:50-11:00	Segment VI: Sharing (Writing) (whole class)

11:00-11:50	Gym
11:50-12:40	Math
12:40-1:20	Lunch
1:20-2:00	Art
2:00-2:40	Integrated Unit (Science and Social Studies)
2:40-3:10	Vocabulary Building, Oral Language Experiences, and Spelling
3:15	Dismissal

Figure 3.1

What I like most about this schedule is that students are empowered learners who have a voice in the classroom. They learn to protect their learning environment and develop pride and a sense of responsibility for their work. Added to all that, the literacy block runs smoothly and students excel as readers, writers, and thinkers.

CLASSROOM LAYOUT: HELPFUL HINTS

It is imperative to pay attention to the physical layout of your classroom. A good physical environment is a boon to successful classroom management. Arrange the meeting area/classroom library away from the classroom door, with children's backs to the door when seated in the area. In this way, you are ensuring students can't see people who pass by, keeping distractions to a minimum.

Put a large rug in the classroom meeting area. There is nothing more uncomfortable for students than sitting on a bare floor. They need to be comfortable so they can engage in learning. Allow space around the rug for students to easily get to and enter the class meeting area.

Ensure all students know where materials and supplies are kept. In the first few weeks of school, set up routines to make sure all materials are returned to their correct places. At the beginning of the year, end sessions five minutes early and supervise the return of all materials and supplies.

When setting up tables, have a maximum of six students per table. If you have a particularly talkative group of children who find staying on task difficult, limit the number in each group to four. Also, try to have a gender balance at each table.

Set up another small rug as an additional meeting area for small-group instructions, such as guided reading and writing sessions. In this way, the meeting area remains open as a place for five or six children to engage in independent activities. Figure 3.2 presents my classroom layout.

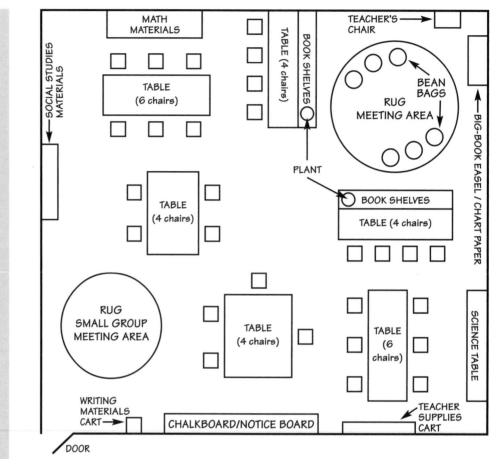

Figure 3.2

Now that you have received tips on how to set up and manage your schedule, check the schedules provided on pages 46–47 and in the Appendix to get ideas for your own scheduling. Remember that your schedule does not have to look exactly like the ones in the Appendix. It does have to reflect an appropriate amount of uninterrupted time focused on teaching literacy and knowing each student as a reader, writer, speller, and thinker.

CHAPTER 4

READING IN GRADES FOUR, FIVE, AND SIX

> There is no single way to read well, though there is a prime reason why we should read. Information is endlessly available to us; where shall wisdom be found? If you are fortunate, you encounter a particular teacher who can help, yet finally you are alone, going on without further mediation . . . finally there is no method but yourself.
>
> (from *How to Read and Why* ©2000 by Harold Bloom)

This chapter addresses how you can become the particular teacher who can help a child become a reader. Becoming a reader means choosing the path of lifelong reading for oneself. The purpose of reading is actually to discover oneself. Teachers of reading don't teach to change students; rather, they lead them along a path of independence, so that students discover who they are. Children should read for the same reason that Bloom says adults should read: to enlarge their lives.

Reading is basically a solitary journey. As you read this page, you are alone even if you are surrounded by other people. Only you know the print you see and "hear" the words resonate in your brain. Even a text listened to is internalized differently by each person. Of course, the best classrooms are communities of learners where children share in the literacy they have created. Sharing is essential. The reading process itself, however, is internal. That's why fourth-, fifth-, and sixth-grade teachers must strive to know each reader individually.

Begin the daunting task of teaching reading to approximately 24 fourth, fifth, or sixth graders in your classroom with three basic steps. These steps will help students who are not reading become readers, while helping those children who are already reading to develop their reading skills and strategies to their fullest potential.

Step 1: Match students to books they can read.
Step 2: Increase the volume of reading in your classroom.
Step 3: Teach reading.

STEP 1: MATCH STUDENTS WITH BOOKS THEY CAN READ

Matching students with books they can read is one of the most important jobs of the fourth-, fifth-, and sixth-grade teacher. Research indicates that your students need to read on a level that is under their control (Report of the National Reading Panel, 2000). They may benefit from challenging text, especially instructional level material under your mediation, but the level of books they are matched with should not be frustrating. When I observe exemplary literacy classrooms, I invariably see children matched appropriately to the books they have in their hands. They often have book bags or book boxes at their desks filled with choices of books they can read. There is usually some visible evidence of leveled texts present in the classroom. Small, guided reading groups are organized where students are appropriately matched with the instructional texts they are using. Children are never being forced to read books that are so hard that frustration or resentfulness is evident.

Fourth-, fifth- and sixth-grade teachers use one set of criteria to match students with books for independent reading and a second set of criteria for the guided reading or instruction that requires the teacher's mediation.

The text matches for INDEPENDENT READING when the student:

Recognizes 95% to 100% of the words accurately.

Accurately comprehends and retells the story or content adequately or completely.

Responds appropriately to comprehension questions such as: *What is the problem in this story? What information are you gathering about setting, characters, and so on? What is happening? What are you finding out? How is the information being presented? How did the story or section end?*

The text matches for GUIDED READING (instructional level) when the student:

Recognizes 90% to 95% of the words accurately.

Accurately comprehends and retells the story or content adequately with guidance.

Responds appropriately to comprehension questions with some guidance.

Rereads the selection independently at the conclusion of the guided reading session.

ASSESSMENT ACTIVITY: THE FIVE FINGER TEST

The Five Finger Test is a simple and very effective quick check to see whether a particular text is a good match for a student's independent reading level. It is based on the theoretical work of Emmett Betts who developed guidelines for independent, instructional, and frustration reading levels in the 1940s (Betts, 1946). These levels still make sense today. As with any quick check, it's an initial indicator, not the final word, as to whether a text really is appropriate for a student. Consequently, it should be used with some flexibility. Asking a student to read a more lengthy passage from the text and to retell the story or answer comprehension questions provides additional verification of a text's suitability for independent reading.

Here's how it works: Choose a representative section of continuous text that is around 100 words in length. Take a quick estimate of the number of words per line. Divide 100 by this number. For example, if there are approximately 10 words per line, the calculation is 100 (words) ÷ 10 (words per line) = 10 (lines). The quotient will equal the number of lines you must count down to get a 100-word sample. In the example given here, one would count down 10 lines of text to identify approximately 100 words in a section of text.

Have the student read the 100-word passage aloud. Raise a finger every time he or she misses a word. If you raise more than five fingers, sight word recognition for the passage is less than 95%, an indication that the book is probably too hard. Use common sense. If the passage contains an obscure word that is repeatedly miscued, choose another 100-word sample: You might say, "This passage has a lot of repetitions of that very hard word. Let's take another sample." Students who pass the Five Finger Test are likely to be able to handle the book independently. (Note: You may use the Ten Finger Test for instructional level material.)

I teach fourth, fifth, and sixth graders the Five Finger Test at the beginning of the year. We use it often in book selection conferences. They even like to use it themselves, as a self-test to see if the book they have selected seems too hard or just right.

Remember to adapt the Five Finger Test when necessary. I often find readers who are passionate about a topic and willing to put the time and effort into reading a book that is actually too hard for them. Nonfiction often calls for flexibility since much nonfiction is gleaned for information and not read page by page from beginning to end.

START THE YEAR BY MATCHING STUDENTS TO TEXTS THEY CAN READ

Matching students with texts is so important that many teachers are having success by taking several weeks at the beginning of the year to get the independent reading component of the reading workshop going before they begin guided reading instruction. Since the expectation is that students will often be reading independently while you are occupied with small guided reading groups, it makes sense to establish independent reading routines first. Remember, if students are thumbing through texts or just pretending to read, it may be an indication that the book they have is too difficult. It's certainly an indication that independent reading is not working.

Consider beginning the year by setting up the classroom for independent reading and establishing routines. Give students both ownership and shared responsibility for physically organizing the classroom library. (This activity will help acquaint them with the books in your room.) Make book bags or personal book boxes (cardboard boxes with each student's name on them). Have students help arrange your classroom collection of leveled texts.

At the beginning of the year, put a lot of effort into guiding their selections. Make charts such as "How to Choose Just Right Books." Initially, you may assign books to their book bags: "Sean, here are three books I have chosen just for you. Try them out and I'll conference with you to find out which ones you like."

Once the initial assignments are made, begin meeting with groups of four to six students and conference with each child. Check to see if the initial assignments are a good fit.

Model how to self-select appropriate books, skimming a book to judge if it's interesting and easy enough to handle. Set up routines for selecting new books for the book bag, rotating the schedule so that only about six students are selecting new books at a time. Decide upon a reasonable number of books they can check out at one time. Conduct mini-lessons and establish high expectations for the volume of reading expected over the year. Begin book talks, engaging students with literature. At the end of several weeks, a visitor may walk into your classroom and observe 25 children with book bags reading independently for a sustained period of time. Your reading workshop is off and running! You are beginning to know each student as a reader.

AVOID MATCHING STUDENTS WITH TEXTS THEY CAN'T READ

Let's look at an example of when students are spending their time with mismatched texts. I am fortunate to visit hundreds of classrooms across the country every year. Many classrooms I visit aren't limited at all: resources are available, students seem to be hard at work, and teachers are diligent. But students are not reading. The crux of the problem seems to be that students have neither been matched with books they can read nor given time to read in school. Too often they are spending time with books they can't read!

Here's an example: What if children come to you having spent most of their reading time in third grade with books like the third-grade science book? What if most of their time reading has been in round-robin reading lessons out of a basal—a format that allows for very little actual reading time—with little opportunity to read books of their own choosing or books they can handle independently? They may already be going down a path that disenfranchises them as readers.

During a recent consulting stint, I visited eight elementary schools in a large school district to observe and work with students and teachers. I interviewed 16 third graders selected at random. I asked the students to bring the books they were reading to the interview. Some of the students showed up with book bags and perfect matches for independent reading. But in other schools, several of the students brought their science book and explained that the science book was a book they were spending a lot of time reading this year. Curious to discover what I might learn, I asked all 16 third graders to read the following random passage from the third grade science text they brought to the interview:

Weather

Earth's atmosphere is more than 160 kilometers (100 mi) thick. But weather takes place only in the 10 kilometers (6 mi) of air directly above Earth's surface.

Everybody talks about the weather, but what is it? *Weather* is what is happening in the atmosphere at a certain place. Temperature, wind, and precipitation are all parts of weather. There would be no weather without the sun. The sun's heat causes clouds, winds, and precipitation to form.

Meteorologists are scientists who study weather and the atmosphere. They measure and record changes in air. These changes help them know if the weather will be sunny or stormy.

(from Harcourt Science ©2000, Grade 3)

None of the 16 children were struggling as readers, but many of them *did* struggle with this text. Only two of the 16 could read and comprehend the passage independently. Not one fully comprehended *precipitation* without my mediation. In addition, several of them sacrificed fluency in order to sound out *atmosphere, kilometers,* temperature, or *meteorologists,* but mental effort spent decoding these challenging words soaked up their attention and interrupted the flow of the passage. Even though some of them decoded the words correctly, they lost the meaning. The effort spent sounding out words drained the life out of comprehension. Good readers recognize most words on sight and attach the spoken word to the printed word automatically, freeing up the frontal lobes for comprehension (Moats, 2000). For most of the students I interviewed, the unknown words eroded their comprehension.

Some of the students lacked the background knowledge to fully comprehend the passage. For example, they miscued on the abbreviation for miles, losing the gist of the passage. There wasn't anything wrong with most of these readers. The problem was that the science text wasn't a good match for their independent reading level. Yet the students reported to me that the science text "was a book that they spent a lot of time reading." Richard Allington passionately describes this phenomenon as ". . . teachers dragging children kicking and screaming through science texts!" He points out that books such as science texts are often written about two grade levels above the designated grade level of the text. These books are thick, uninteresting, and hard. Many of the students cannot read them without mediation. Children do not become lifelong readers by spending most of their time with books that are thick, uninteresting, and hard (Allington, 2000)!

Ask teachers and they will explain to you why children in their classroom bring their science text when asked to bring the books they are spending most of their time reading: "We have to teach science. It's required in the standard course of study," or "Most of the passages on the end-of-grade test are content passages." These teachers, faced with the stark realities of high-stakes testing, are diligent in their efforts to meet some of the unrealistic and unreasonable demands they face on a daily basis. Often they are doing their best with what's given to or required of them. But the reality of the situation is that reading is not occurring when science texts are the main books students have in their hands. The science text for third grade may be a mismatch for many third-grade students' independent reading.

And it's not just the science text. One of the third graders I interviewed pulled a familiar news weekly from his book bag. He told me he had been reading an article about the presidential election. I asked him to tell me about his favorite section. He chose an article explaining how George W. Bush picked former U.S. Secretary of Defense Richard Cheney to be his vice presidential running mate. The child didn't understand what "former," "Secretary of Defense," or "vice presidential" meant. When he reread the article to me, he had to sound out *representatives, administration, Republican,* and *presidential.*

"She (the teacher) told us we could use this during DEAR (Drop Everything and Read) time," he reported. Then he confessed. "But I wasn't really reading it—just flipping through the pages. I had to do it for 20 minutes," he sighed. "It was boring!"

When students are developing as readers, the sophistication of the text they have control of as a reader increases from year to year. Using leveled text gives credence to the fact that some books make more demands on the reader than others and to the fact that your students should reflect growth in the level of text that they can read.

Use of leveled texts is a signal that you are matching children to books they can read. A full explanation of the possibilities for using leveled texts for independent reading, assessment, and instruction is described later in this chapter.

STEP 2: INCREASE THE VOLUME OF READING IN YOUR CLASSROOM

I met with fourth-grade teachers in a large suburban district. As we began to discuss how to improve the reading of students in their classrooms, we made a startling discovery. There was a huge discrepancy in the expectations of the volume of reading students should do. I asked the teachers to choose a number that best represented the number of books fourth graders in their classroom would complete this year including actual reading in class and reading at home. Forty-five teachers submitted their estimates anonymously. Their estimates were evenly spread across a continuum. To their astonishment, the range of the number of books they expected most fourth graders to complete ranged from 12 to over 40! Imagine the difference in potential for literacy growth in two fourth-grade classrooms, one in which students are reading 12 books a year, the other in which students are reading over 40 books!

I believe that one of most powerful changes in literacy education in the last 20 years is that we have increased the volume of reading and writing. Fountas and Pinnell, for example, expect that fourth through sixth graders should read about one chapter book per week or "about 40 books per year" (Fountas and Pinnell, 2001. *Guiding Readers and Writers: Grades 3–6,* p. 176). New York State standards document, *The English Language Arts Standards,* includes an "extensive reading standard" requiring students to read 25 books per year. Richard Allington calls for "a 90-minute volume standard for daily in-school reading" (Allington, 2001, p. 40). One effective way to increase the volume of reading among students in your classroom is to build in a block of time for sustained, supervised, independent reading during each school day. Increasing the amount of time that students read in the classroom is not a new idea. Allington stressed the importance of reading and writing frequently over 20 years ago (1977).

Considerable reading research and theory support the idea of increasing the volume of reading in school. It is important to note, however, that The National Reading Panel found "independent silent reading is not an effective practice when used as the only type of reading instruction . . . " (p. 13). You can't simply have children reading independently in your classroom; you have to *teach* reading. When students read on their own in school, teachers should monitor, evaluate, and provide feedback.

GIVE STUDENTS ACCESS TO BOOKS

One way to increase your students' volume of reading is to give them easy access to books. Two simple ideas greatly increase the access students have to books in your classroom: book bags and classroom libraries. Fourth-, fifth-, and sixth-grade teachers have reported to me that providing book bags and/or expanding their classroom libraries result in greater increases in the volume of reading among their students, and, as a result, increase reading achievement.

UTLIZE BOOK BAGS, BOOK BOXES

Book bags or book boxes are a simple solution for making "just right books" accessible all day long in school. These bags and boxes range from sturdy store-bought canvas bags or small backpacks to shopping bags, shoeboxes, or large plastic, sealable bags adapted for this purpose. I like to visit classrooms where book bags are as essential to the child as a hammer and nails are to the carpenter. Often book bags are at the child's desk and at appropriate times move with the child from one location to the next to facilitate independent reading. Students adapt to using book bags easily. This system is infinitely better than having them stampede a section of shelving or row of boxes on the window ledge. Book bags should be within arms reach at all times for students to access when they finish a project early.

Book bags don't work well when the books in the bag are not a good match for the reader or when few of the books are self-selected. I think book bags should include light as well as heavier reading. It's acceptable for students to be reading several books at the same time. A good rule of thumb is to have enough reading material in a book bag so that the reader might hypothetically be occupied with several reading choices for several hours of uninterrupted reading.

CREATE A CLASSROOM LIBRARY

The library, often the epicenter of the classroom, should be carpeted and multifunctional so it can serve as a whole-class meeting area, a refuge for independent readers, and a meeting place for a book club or reading buddies.

Fourth-, fifth-, and sixth-grade classroom libraries often contain up to 1,000 titles. There is evidence of leveled texts but other collections are grouped by genre, author, or topic. Teachers often use creativity to build their own impressive classroom collections. Here are ideas for expanding the classroom library:

- Borrow in bulk from local libraries.
- Collect used books brought in by students.
- Conduct book fairs.
- Pool classroom orders to earn free books.
- Ask parents to purchase books to be placed in the classroom in honor of their children.
- Ask community groups to donate books.
- Sponsor school-wide competitions (a penny drive, for example) to raise money for classroom libraries.
- Recycle children's books collected by high-school service clubs.
- Find a local sponsor to help build your own classroom library.

Whatever you do, give yourself plenty of time. Extensive classroom libraries aren't built overnight.

STEP 3: TEACH READING

This section provides a checklist to help you critique your effectiveness as a teacher of reading.

Do you know each student as a reader? Do you observe and assess each of your students individually? What is his or her reading level? Can you describe his or her reading habits? What are his or her strengths and weaknesses? Is comprehension on a surface level or does he or she think deeply about what is being read? Can he or she analyze, synthesize, and evaluate? What can be determined about the student's fluency and reading rate? What books is he or she reading? Can you comment on the quantity and quality of the reading? What are his or her reading habits out of school? Throughout the year the following strategies should be observed and assessed for each student.

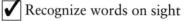

☑ Recognize words on sight

☑ Solve unknown words

☑ Monitor and self-correct

☑ Maintain fluency

☑ Maintain an appropriate reading rate

☑ Read for different purposes: skimming, scanning, and gathering information

☑ Make predictions while reading

☑ Visualize or create images

☑ Summarize

☑ Infer

☑ Analyze

☑ Synthesize

☑ Critique or evaluate

☑ Make text-to-self, text-to-text, and text-to-world knowledge connections

Changes to expect from year to year are the level of sophistication of the text and the demands of higher levels of text on the reader. For example, both fourth-grade level readers and fifth-grade level readers use making predictions, making inferences, and synthesizing information strategies. The fifth-grade reader is using these strategies with more difficult text at a higher level of sophistication. Readers at both fourth- and fifth-grade levels might be assessed for comprehension and strategy use, such as summarizing and making inferences. However, the fourth-grade level reader might read material such as Beverly Cleary's *Beezus and Ramona* (beginning fourth-grade level), while the fifth-grade level reader might read Jim Murphy's *The Great Fire* (fifth-grade level). Because of the difference in the levels of the text, full comprehension of these stories places very different demands on the reader. The story structure in *Beezus and Ramona* is straightforward and concrete as compared to the abstract sequencing of eyewitness accounts interwoven to tell the story of *The Great Fire*. Contrast the books' concept and vocabulary loads. In *Beezus and Ramona*, readers encounter words such as *exasperating, embroidering, harmonica, inhaling, defiantly,* and *obligingly,* but they encounter even harder words and concepts in *The Great Fire*, such as *extinguished, inferno, privation, anarchist, indulged, diatribe, scapegoat,* and *demoralization.*

Contrasting the demands of *Beezus and Ramona* and *The Great Fire* may provide some insight into qualitative changes in how children think as fourth-grade readers versus fifth- or sixth-grade readers. One might postulate from Piaget's stages of development that readers reaching 10 and 11 years of age (which includes many fourth graders) are likely to be nearing the end of the period and approximate age range for concrete operations. I speculate that much of what they handle well as readers may require thinking "limited to concrete phenomena and their own past experiences; that is, thinking that is not abstract." (Bjorklund, 1995, p. 62) In my view, a book such as *Beezus and Ramona,* with many referents to the fourth grader's real life, requires this level of thinking, as opposed to reading that requires more abstract thinking. For example, it may be difficult for many fourth-grade readers to shift back and forth in a story or informational text told from many complex perspectives.

The demands of *The Great Fire* are larger by comparison. This book requires the reader "to introspect about their own thought processes and, generally . . . think abstractly" (Bjorklund, 1995, p. 62). There is much more room for the reader to make complex hypotheses during its reading. *The Great Fire* requires a great deal of internal reflection. There is more opportunity in the text for complex deductive reasoning (moving from the general to the specific) that is not limited to what the reader has experienced but includes new hypothetical possibilities. *The Great Fire* also presents possibilities for complex inductive reasoning (moving from specific observations to broad generalizations) as in the last chapter, "Myth and Reality." Here the reader must consider three complex theories about who was at fault for the Chicago fire, weigh all the evidence, and draw his or her own conclusion as to who was really responsible for the colossal disaster.

What may be assessed and taught at the fourth-, fifth-, and sixth-grade levels is often determined by the content of the text. For example, *Beezus and Ramona* lends itself to teaching and assessing strategies such as making predictions, drawing conclusions, analyzing character development, predicting feelings and reactions, making inferences from concrete evidence, and synthesizing concrete information. *The Great Fire,* on the other hand, is a powerful text for focusing on recognizing cause and effect, sequencing events, distinguishing fact from opinion, reading maps, and making inferences and syntheses that require abstract thinking.

As you consider observation and assessment of each of your students for all of the strategies in the checklist, the challenge is not as daunting as you might think when you consider that both observing and teaching are everyday activities for the teacher. It's what you will be doing every day in your two to two-and-one-half hour literacy block. Assessment and instruction will be ongoing, primarily taking place in small guided-reading groups of four to six students where the teacher has the opportunity to observe the reader with instructional level material in various contexts. Teachers also assess individuals in whole-class reading lessons as well as in occasional individual conferences. These everyday assessments will inform your instruction and help you guide each reader.

In addition to ongoing assessment, instruments such as standardized tests, the state testing program, informal reading inventories, and miscue analyses provide further information about each student as a reader.

FOSTER INDEPENDENT READING

Teachers need to pay attention to the volume of reading in school. Literacy programs are not working in schools if we end up with children who *can* read but *don't* read. Reading in school correlates to higher reading achievement and is necessary for developing the habit of reading—a habit that leads to lifelong reading. Independent reading in school should be monitored by the teacher and should include self-selection of books under the teacher's guidance.

Research supports having students spend time reading. Allington's research findings over a number of years indicate that higher-achieving students on average read three times as much each week in school as their lower-achieving classmates (Allington, 1977, 1980,1983, 1984; Allington and Mcgill-Franzen, 1989). The Anderson, Wilson, and Fielding study (1988) found fifth graders at the 90th percentile in reading achievement averaging 40 minutes of reading per day out of school compared with less than two minutes of reading per day by fifth graders at the 10th percentile. In a study involving 165 fifth- and sixth-grade students in 50-minute reading blocks, Taylor, Frye, and Maruyama (1990) found that reading blocks devoting more time to actual reading contributed significantly to individual reading growth. There is no doubt that increasing the amount of reading that students do in school correlates to higher reading achievement (Report of the National Reading Panel, 2000).

FORM SMALL-GROUP AND WHOLE-CLASS INSTRUCTIONAL GROUPS

Guided reading is an instructional session involving explicit teaching to help students develop reading strategies. The teacher first selects the material to be used. Then the teacher *guides* a student or students while reading and instructs using the material being read. The lesson has a purpose—developing comprehension strategies, developing prediction strategies, building fluency, etc. While guided reading generally takes place in small groups, teachers may also conduct a guided-reading lesson with the whole class or with an individual in a conference. A whole-class Directed Reading Thinking Activity, for example, is guided reading. (See pages 63–64 for an explanation of the DRTA.)

The term *guided reading* has been used by different authors to describe very different kinds of instructional frameworks. In *Guided Reading the Four-Blocks™ Way* (2000), Patricia Cunningham, Dorothy Hall, and James Cunningham use this term to describe one of four daily 30 to 40 minute blocks of instruction for a framework they recommend primarily for grades one through three. (Time allocations change for their recommendations for four blocks in the upper grades.) In this model of guided reading, ". . . children are not put in fixed ability groups, the instruction is made as multilevel as possible so that average, struggling, and excelling students all learn to read and write at the highest possible level." (p. 18) Their guided-reading lessons have a before, during, and after reading phase. (p. 22) Rather than match students with instructional level material, the teacher alternates average reading level and easier reading level materials with whole-class multilevel groups. On some days their guided reading is organized in a "three-ring circus" where the whole class is reading the same material simultaneously in one of three formats: students may choose to read the text with the teacher, by themselves, or with a partner (p. 182). This version of guided reading, which Cunningham, et al. illustrate as a possibility for a fifth-grade classroom (p. 15), bears little resemblance to the Fountas and Pinnell model.

In *Guiding Readers and Writers Grades 3-6*, Fountas and Pinnell define *guided reading* as one of the three kinds of reading and response that occurs in a reading workshop—guided reading, independent reading, and literature study. Their definition of the guided-reading component is as follows:

> *Guided reading,* in which a small group of students with similar reading strategies work with you to learn more about reading. You select a text at an appropriate level, introduce it, and provide supportive teaching that helps the group understand what reading is and how it works.
>
> (Fountas and Pinnell, 2001, p. 40)

In the Fountas and Pinnell model, guided-reading groups, sometimes pulled together on a temporary basis, are small groups of students who share similar learning needs. Selections for guided reading are generally short enough to complete in one or two meetings and most of the reading is silent and followed by discussion. The teacher may occasionally ask individuals to read aloud, checking for oral fluency or decoding strategies. In the Fountas and Pinnell description of guided reading, the teacher teaches important concepts and principles to small homogeneous groups of readers and "selects text that offers appropriate supports and challenges" (p. 41). They distinguish *guided reading* from *literature study* in which "small heterogeneous groups" work with the teacher to study a text or sets of related texts (p. 41). Students in literature study groups don't necessarily have to be able to read the book but may experience it by being read to and listening. In their model, *literature study* is synonymous with *book club, literature circle, literature discussion group,* and *response group* (p. 47).

As these two different frameworks suggest, there is great room for flexibility for how you implement the particulars of reading instruction in your classroom. For example, literature study could be done with the whole class, with a small guided-reading group, or even as an independent literacy activity by individuals who meet in a book club while the teacher is meeting with a small guided-reading group. Likewise, read alouds followed by book talks, or shared reading in which the teacher and students share in the reading of a piece, might take place in a whole-class block or in small groups. While the Fountas and Pinnell framework divides reading workshop into independent reading, guided reading, and literature study, other similar models divide it into "self-selected reading," guided reading (with children not being guided by the teacher concurrently engaging in independent, partner, or small-group literacy activities), and whole-class teaching. There may be advantages in using one framework or the other, but in whatever framework you choose, you must observe and teach *each reader.* Both large and small instructional groupings are effective in fourth-, fifth-, and sixth-grade classrooms.

Why form both small and large instructional reading groups? Forming large groups or whole-class instruction is efficient. Large groups take full advantage of the social context of reading. A whole-class read aloud and book talk, for example, allow all members of the classroom community of learners to respond to the same text. Modeling, demonstrations, and discussion allow comprehension and fluency to grow out of whole class experiences. On the other hand, much of the nitty-gritty of reading instruction may derive from work with small groups of readers.

Suppose you have 12 fifth graders, including a student we'll call Rose, who all read on the same level. There is a disadvantage to grouping all 12 students in a large guided-reading group. Even if the text and the instructional goals are the same for all 12 students, you will find it hard to know what Rose is thinking when she is buried in your observation of all 12 students at once. How is she responding to the selection? What specifically are you observing about Rose during this 20-minute guided-reading lesson? Will Rose get a chance, with 11 other participants, to respond to this selection as you mediate the reading? Is Rose solving unknown words and self-correcting? Will you have an opportunity to check Rose's fluency as she reads aloud to confirm a prediction? Can Rose summarize, make inferences, or make connections? Can she take this piece to a level of comprehension requiring analysis, synthesis, or critiquing?

Many best practice classrooms are moving to small, guided-reading groups even if the groups meet every other day as opposed to meeting with the teacher every day. Small, guided-reading groups connect the teacher with each individual reader for observation and instruction. The advantage of the small, guided-reading group (four to six students) is that you can observe, monitor, and mediate aspects such as the ones mentioned above, for each student. In addition, each student will be able to respond to the selection in ways that you suggest, for example, make an inference called for in the text or a text-to-self connection.

Teachers often form three or four guided-reading groups in their reading workshop and meet with three groups each day. If groups are small, it's sufficient to meet with some groups every other day while more needy groups are met daily. Knowing each student individually and meeting each student's needs is more important than daily guided-reading sessions with all four reading groups.

USE VARIED TEACHING METHODS

The scope of this book cannot provide an all-inclusive treatment on teaching reading methodology. I would, however, like to provide a few concrete models of teaching techniques to demonstrate what is effective. With appropriate variation, the following three teaching models may be used to guide reading in whole-class reading groups as well as in small guided-reading groups.

TEACHING ACTIVITY: DRTA (DIRECTED READING THINKING ACTIVITY)

Methodologies of teaching comprehension in guided reading have been around for a long time. One effective technique is the DRTA (Directed Reading Thinking Activity), highly touted by outstanding contemporary scholars of reading comprehension like Dorsey Hammond at Oakland University in Detroit (Hammond and Raphael, 1999).

DRTA is a technique developed by Russell Stauffer, a Professor of Reading Education at the University of Delaware (1968, 1969). The purpose of the technique is to guide or direct the reader's thinking as he or she reads so that the reader learns to make predictions and then rereads to confirm while self-monitoring for understanding. During the reading process, the reader is constantly making hypotheses, predicting and confirming, or changing predictions, based on what he or she finds out from reading. The predicting and confirming drives the reader's thinking throughout the reading process. It may encompass higher-order thinking skills such as inferring, synthesizing, analyzing, and critiquing.

The basic structure of a DRTA is as follows:

- Select unseen material written at the readers' instructional level.
- Divide the selection into logical stopping places for predicting and discussion.
- Have the readers read silently to the stopping place: "When you get to the bottom of page 3, put your finger in the book to hold your place, close the book, and look up to let me know you are done." (Closing the book helps the reader avoid the temptation of reading ahead.)
- After reading a section silently, the readers discuss what they found out and predict what they think will happen next.
- The teacher then directs the readers to read to the next logical stopping place and continue the procedure.
- When the readers reach a logical stopping point, the teacher often asks a reader to go back and read aloud the section that supports what he or she found out. This provides the teacher an opportunity to monitor an individual's oral fluency as well as comprehension. It also gives readers practice with skimming and scanning techniques.
- The cycle continues until the end of the lesson.

DRTAs are often conducted in small, guided-reading groups with all participants reading the same material silently.

A variation of the DRTA, used in whole-group contexts or when there is only one copy of the book for multiple readers to share, is the Directed Listening Thinking Activity. Here the teacher reads the material out loud, pausing at logical stopping points to have the listeners predict, discuss, and confirm. It's a variation of a read aloud and book talk format.

I often do DLTAs with micro-texts, such as *When Pigasso Met Mootisse* by Nina Laden for whole-class instruction in comprehension to teach the strategy of making predictions. I choose micro-texts that are well written, engaging, and that demand little time. This allows the main focus of the lesson to proceed expediently. Ralph Fletcher demonstrates the same effectiveness of using micro-texts in writing workshop by using these short eminently readable picture books to model various strategies (Fletcher and Portalupi, 1998). Here's an outline of my Directed Listening Thinking Activity for a whole-class session with 25 fourth graders.

DLTA: *When Pigasso Met Mootisse* **by Nina Laden**

Fourth graders find *When Pigasso Met Mootisse* funny and engaging. It's written on a fourth- or fifth-grade level and allows for extended independent reading at the conclusion of the lesson. There are many possibilities for extending this piece, an abundance of humor, and intellectual challenge. Rather than reading aloud the last section of the book, "The True Story of Picasso and Matisse," I save this part for independent or buddy reading and use it as a literacy activity for students to work on independently while I'm working with other students in guided-reading groups.

First I call the whole-class reading group together and begin the lesson by introducing the book:

DLTA: *When Pigasso Met Mootisse* by Nina Laden

Gentry: Boys and girls, you all know I love modern art. Today I'm going to read aloud one of my favorite books to share with fourth graders, *When Pigasso Met Mootisse* by Nina Laden. Our book talk will be in the format of a DLTA. Listen carefully. This story is full of very hilarious puns. I think you'll also enjoy the illustrations. At the end of the story, we'll see if you notice a clever trick the author uses with the illustrations. Listen to the blurb to find out more about the story.

Gentry reads the back cover blurb.

Text: When Pigasso met Mootisse—or was it when Mootisse met Pigasso? —what begins as a neighborly overture between a painterly pig and an artsy cow escalates into a monumental modern art mess.

Gentry reads the first section and the listeners learn that Pigasso's talent is spreading "throughout the pig provinces" and that Mootisse is "getting famous in the cattle community. There weren't many households that didn't own a 'Moosterpiece'" (p. 5). Then Gentry pauses and asks for the first prediction.

Gentry: What do you think is going to happen?

The next section confirms that both characters decide to move to "a peaceful place where they could paint without distractions." Coincidentally, they become neighbors in the country with houses facing each other. At first they are friendly. Gentry stops at the second logical stopping point, page 10.

Text: . . . soon things begin to change.

Gentry: Well, what do you think will happen now?

The reading confirms that they have a feud. The remarkable story of friendship, disagreement, and conflict/resolution unfolds. Gentry continues to read aloud, stopping at logical stopping points to allow the listeners to test their hypotheses, make predictions, and verify them.

Gentry: What will happen when they begin to criticize each other's painting style? How does their feud play out? What is the new problem in the story? What do you think will happen next? What is the resolution?

After the read aloud of *When Pigasso Met Mootisse*, one might enter my classroom and see students in pairs or independently reading and viewing the text, while I am in another part of the room with a guided-reading group. Creative teachers come up with wonderful literacy extensions for books like *When Pigasso Met Mootisse*, such as a writing workshop where students write humorous pieces using puns, creating stories by turning the historical personalities they are studying into animal characters, or a mini-lesson during writing workshop. (A mini-lesson on word choice taken from *When Pigasso Met Mootisse* is modeled on pages 78–80.) There are excellent connections to literacy with opportunities for artistic expression; however, I do not allow artistic expression to substitute for literacy activities during reading workshop. (I often remind teachers, "No one ever learned to read making log cabins out of ice-cream sticks!")

TEACHING ACTIVITY: READ ALOUDS WITH BOOK TALKS

Read alouds with book talks are often used in whole-class instruction to model reading and thinking strategies appropriate for grades four, five, and six. I've developed a model for fifth grade with *The Great Fire* by Jim Murphy.

Read Aloud: *The Great Fire* by Jim Murphy

Gentry: Welcome to our whole-class book share. Today I'm going to read sections of an extraordinary book, *The Great Fire* by Jim Murphy. It's one of my favorites. Mr. Murphy, an award-winning author, was rummaging around in an antique bookstore in Chicago when he came across a copy of the first book ever written about the great Chicago fire. It was published in December, 1871, only two months after the fire. The book included eyewitness accounts of the disaster. To write *The Great Fire*, the author conducted research, studied old maps, and wove a collection of survivors' personal accounts into an astonishing chronicle of what actually happened from October 8 through October 10, 1871. The fire virtually wiped out the whole city of Chicago and left almost 100,000 people homeless.

This is a striking book—full of actual photographs and engravings from the era—including scenes from before and after the fire. The book displays maps of the city, showing most of the streets exactly the same as they are today. As you read this book, you'll be able to use the maps to follow the progression of the fire as it spread across the city.

Time limitations present a problem for fourth-, fifth-, and sixth-grade teachers who love to share literature in their classrooms. *The Great Fire* is 144 pages long—not long by chapter book standards, but perhaps too long to read aloud in class. Reading the entire volume aloud, allowing time for book talks and discussion is an inordinate amount of shared reading time. With this text, I share enough of the story to pique interest, teach the historical significance of the event, sample the author's style, and experience the aesthetic enjoyment of the riveting, nonfiction text. I share with my listeners the background needed to understand the final chapter entitled "Myth and Reality," which they later are held accountable to read independently or with the aid of a taped recording.

Jim Murphy uses the voices of a number of eyewitnesses to tell the story, brilliantly interweaving them so that the story unfolds chronologically. The reader follows several characters as they witness the city crumble to ashes over a period of four days.

When I use *The Great Fire* as a read aloud, I read or tell the story of only one of the survivors–12-year-old Claire Innes. (She appears on pages 34-36, 49-52, 55, 58-60, 72, 80-83, 97, 109-112, and 121.)

While I often tell part of the story, I read enough of it so that the listeners develop an appreciation for the author's voice and style as well as an appreciation for Claire's own voice, presented in samples of her written account of the event.

The heat and dry air had left 12-year-old Claire Innes tired and listless all day. She went to bed sometime between eight and eight-thirty only to be startled awake later when a horse-andwagon clattered past her window at high speed. This was followed by loud voices from the street below her window . . .

"I was only half-awake and not inclined to get up when I heard a man outside say that a fire was burning in the West Division. Father went to the door and asked about the fire and the man repeated what he had told his companions, but this time he added that the fire was a big one and that they were going to have a look at it. Father came inside and said something to Mother. . . . His voice did not sound unusual, [so] I turned over and closed my eyes again." (pp. 34-36)

Claire didn't sleep for long. Her mother aroused her as the family, two younger brothers and a baby sister, were readied for the evacuation. Each took a bundle of clothes and food, and they left the house and headed down Clark Street toward the bridge, expecting to find safety across the river. The street was jammed with people. First Claire remembers seeing the fire to the west and the south. Then the sparks and cinders begin to fall on the crowd and the awning of a house catches on fire. The crowd becomes a mob pushing back on them. Claire's father tells them to drop their bundles and hold hands but Claire keeps her bundle. The surge of the crowd begins to sweep them along. Nearby buildings burst into flame and Claire's father picks up the baby. Claire writes that the wind is "terrible, like a storm, and filled with cinders and fire." (p. 58)

At some point Claire, who is still holding the bundle rather than one of her parent's hands, gets in a tussle with a vagrant who tries to grab the bundle away from her. He is pushed away by an onlooker, but when she looks up from the momentary distraction of the tussle, her family is gone. Claire waits, but no one returns. She realizes she's lost and all alone in the panic-stricken mob.

Because Claire is the same age as my listeners, they almost always make text-to-self connections and much discussion ensues. Fifth graders often marvel at the writing of 12-year-old Claire. "The retreat was now a stampede and we were swept along . . . I felt as a leaf . . . in a great rushing river." The reading provides a wonderful model for the students' own writing of eyewitness accounts, which later becomes an extension project in our writing workshop.

The read alouds also allow for extension activities that make good independent literacy activities for individuals or small groups while I'm teaching a small guided-reading group. For example, students do a written response or retelling to verify their understanding of the three theories the last chapter presents regarding who was responsible for the fire.

Another extension is the introduction of the *Survival!* series of eyewitness acounts. Authors K. Duey and K. A. Bale introduce readers to titles, such as *Survival! Earthquake; Survival! Flood*; and *Survival! Hurricane* that they read and share during a daily share time in our reading workshop. This wide and deep reading of eyewitness accounts is excellent preparation for an "eyewitness account" writing project in writing workshop.

TEACHING ACTIVITY: MODELING TEXT-TO-SELF, TEXT-TO-TEXT, AND TEXT-TO-WORLD KNOWLEDGE CONNECTIONS

A technique for enhancing comprehension by activating "mental files" before and during reading grew out of schema theory (Maria, 1990). The technique involves modeling for the reader how to make text-to-self, text-to-text, and text-to-world knowledge connections (Keene and Zimmermann, 1997). Using this strategy, the reader learns to relate new information gleaned from text to his or her own personal experience, to another book he or she has read, or to his or her background knowledge. The procedure works well as a means for getting readers to think more deeply about material they are reading. Modeling connections and book talks help students develop deeper and broader understanding of the ideas or meaning of the text being read. Here are steps to model for students to help them make these connections:

- Conduct a read aloud.
- Explain that you will go back and reread sections of the text.
- Model the way good readers make connections by "thinking aloud," so that your listeners can hear your thoughts as you first read the piece.
- Conduct short (10 or 15 minute) mini-lessons, initially modeling each of the three strategies separately:
  Text-to-self—How the text connected to your own personal experience.
  Text-to-text—How the text connected to another book you have read.
  Text-to-world knowledge—How the text connected to your "world knowledge." Discuss how your background knowledge allowed you to comprehend the piece in a certain way that may not have been possible without the connection you made.
- Make it clear how your thinking helps you understand the text better, keeping examples clear and concise.
- Model first. Delay inviting students to participate until you are sure they understand the "connection" being modeled.

- Invite students to make the type of connection being modeled.
- Use the terminology when discussing the student's independent reading. ("What text-to-self connections are you making in this chapter?")

When modeling the three types of connections, it's good to use a variety of books. Model each type of connection separately. Model over a sustained period of time so that students have a chance to really understand the concept. Generally, you will need to read the text before modeling and think about where to pause and "think aloud." (For more information about using this technique, read *Mosaic of Thought* by Ellin Keene and Susan Zimmermann, 1997.)

WHAT ABOUT LITERATURE GROUPS?

Literature study is part of the reading curriculum in grades four, five, and six. A number of excellent resources guide teachers in conducting literature study groups or book clubs. I particularly recommend *Literature Circles* by Harvey Daniels (2002). He suggests that while some of the elements of literature circles may be intentionally omitted when students are first learning the activity, the following key features should be present in authentic and mature literature circles:

1. Students choose their own reading materials.
2. Groups are small and temporary, based on book choice.
3. Different groups read different books.
4. Groups meet on a regular, predictable schedule.
5. Students take notes to guide their reading and discussion.
6. Discussion topics come from the students.
7. Conversations about books are open and natural.
8. Students rotate in task roles.
9. The teacher is a facilitator, not an instructor.
10. The teacher evaluates observationally and students self-evaluate.
11. Playfulness and fun pervades.
12. New groups form around new reading choices.

Adapted from Daniels, Harvey. 1994 *Literature Circles: Voice and Choice in the Student-Centered Classroom*, Chapter 1, p. 18 (Stenhouse Publishers, ME)

I have visited districts where literature study groups replaced guided reading. While literature study groups are certainly necessary, when conducted in heterogeneous or whole-class groups, they should be a part of the curriculum, not a replacement for small guided-reading groups.

WHAT SHOULD FOURTH, FIFTH, AND SIXTH GRADERS READ?

Harold Bloom says read "to find what truly comes near to you that can be used for weighing and considering" (Bloom, 2000). This is good advice, not only for adults, but also for fourth, fifth, and sixth graders as well. I'm not as interested in discovering a standard of required traditional literature for these grade levels as I am in discovering why and how teachers mediate reading in ways that lead students to become independent readers. Although what students read may influence the particular focus of your instruction, what they read may not be as important as *that* they read and *how*.

Perhaps teachers should be more tolerant of "junk reading," especially when students are making selections for their book bags. I reported earlier how *Konan the Barbarian* comic books opened the door to literacy for one child who grew up to become a professional writer. Millions upon millions of fourth, fifth, and sixth graders have become readers on voracious diets of *Goosebumps* and *Harry Potter*. Most of these readers branch out. I believe R. L. Stein and J. K. Rowling should be revered as literacy heroes for the contribution they have made to reading in America—especially to literacy for fourth, fifth, and sixth graders. The children who devour *Harry Potter* books may one day invite Hamlet or Bloom into their lives.

Adults sometimes show more tolerance of different tastes for the adult reader than for the young reader. Adult readers are not always immersed in high literature such as the classics, poetry, physics, or the Bible. Over 41 million Americans spend $1.35 billion a year on romance novels and over 25% of these readers are college educated. Adults read more romance than the mystery, science fiction, and suspense genres combined (Schultz, 2001).

We should encourage children to read what they enjoy, and display the same tolerance that we do for adults. Children should have the opportunity in school to make some of their own choices for reading material. Both children and adults benefit from broad and deep reading.

I believe the best teachers of reading bring literature that they are passionate about into their classrooms. Children catch the passion! The books I most enjoy sharing with fourth, fifth, and sixth graders reflect my own interests in art and architecture, history, or events in my life. I love to share books about pigs because I grew up on a farm raising feeder litter pigs, and was state champion raiser when I was in fourth grade. Pigs are still a part of my life through books and children seem to enjoy sharing that interest with me.

Whether you are passionate about pigs, Paris, or politics, let the books you share with children reflect your own enthusiasm. The literature you choose to highlight the year of their life they spend with you will stay with some of them long after they leave your classroom. Sharing the books you love is a way of sharing a part of yourself.

CHAPTER 5

WRITING IN GRADES FOUR, FIVE, AND SIX

By Jean Mann with J. Richard Gentry

Author's note: In this chapter, master teacher Jean Mann shares her research on writing development in grades four, five, and six. A theoretical framework for writing benchmarks emerged from this research. These benchmarks are connected to Jean Piaget's concrete operational (7 to 11 years) and formal operational (11 to 16 years) stages of development. (Piaget, 1952, 1969; Bjorklund, 1995). Mann presents research that shows a clear cognitive leap between fourth and fifth grades as many children make the transformation from concrete to formal operational thought.

Mann shows how the genesis of a sophisticated piece of sixth-grade writing can be traced to more elementary structures developed in fifth grade and prior years. She shows how children's writings develop when new structures arise as a result of changes they make in the organization of their mental structure as writers. Their writing development reflects transformations in thought. Mann provides a clear and practical framework for writing benchmarks, as well as teaching activities and strategies. Her work has greatly informed the benchmarks for writing in this book.

FOURTH GRADE: STEP-BY-STEP, CONCRETE OPERATIONS

If you teach fourth-grade writing, the style of Kaisa's story about Merty and Marlow Monkey will be very familiar to you (Figure 5.1). Like other students moving from third to fourth grade, Kaisa enjoys writing about animals, friends, and experiences. Her piece is safe and concrete, and she controls where it goes. A typical beginning fourth grader, kaisa

One morning Marlow woke up after a peaceful sleep. His mom told him to get up and eat his breakfast. He asked his Mom if he could go and play with Merty Monkey. His Mom said he could. He finished his breakfast quickly and ran outside to meet Merty. When he had reached Merty's house he asked Merty if he could play. Merty said yes. Marlow and Merty walked on to there favorite place in the Jungle, the vine swinging place). When they got there, Merty dared Marlow to grab a vine, jump, then grab on to another branch. Marlow thought that would be dangerous. Marlow thought that sounded cool also dangerous. He knew he shouldn't do it but he did it any way. His hands were shaking as he grabbed on the vine. He was very scared! He looked down at the ground and he was terrified! Right when he was in midair about to grab on to the second vine, He fell and hit a very hard rock and his leg hurt badly. His mother and a docter were notified and he was rushed to the hospital and treated. He had broken his leg badly. When he was in the hospital his Mom asked him if he had learned his lesson. He said "yes, don't do things just to be cool do them safely."

Figure 5.1

Kaisa is a concrete thinker. Her story reflects a chronology that she can go back and experience. Each step in time receives equal attention from her.

Kaisa's prewriting, presented in Figure 5.2, shows a single focus. Kaisa used a story map to help her plan her writing. The map is specific, clear-cut, and provides the step-by-step sequence that she needs.

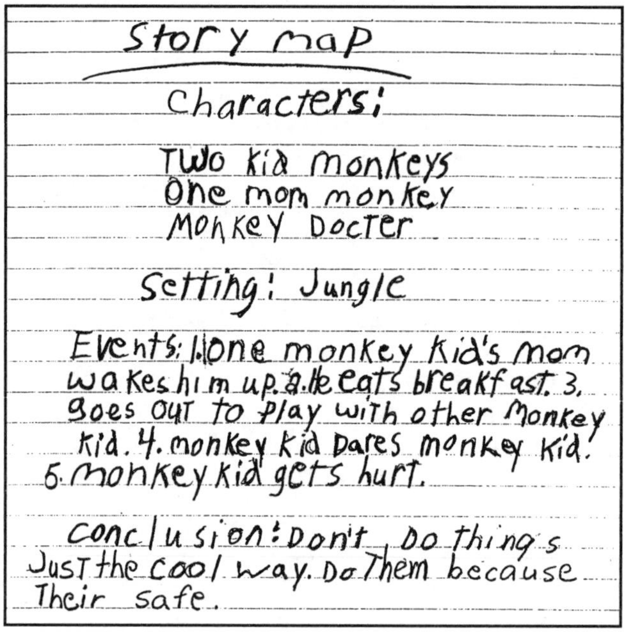

Story map

Characters:

Two kid monkeys
One mom monkey
Monkey Docter

Setting: Jungle

Events: 1. One monkey kid's mom wakes him up. 2. He eats breakfast. 3. goes out to play with other monkey kid. 4. monkey kid Dares monkey kid. 5. monkey kid gets hurt.

Conclusion: Don't Do things Just the cool way. Do Them because Their safe.

Figure 5.2

When Kaisa writes, she pictures each event in her mind, continuing to add on as she moves through each incident. For her, there is very little going back to reread what she has written. Shifting her focus back and forth between reading and writing at this stage would cause too much of an interruption in her thought process. Similarly, she does not choose to stop and reflect upon what she will say next.

Although she would be able to verbally elaborate on details, Kaisa does not include this elaboration within her writing, but rather moves determinably through the chain of events. Thus, there are no paragraphs and few transitions. Shifting gears to change paragraphs or provide transitions may be too demanding for Kaisa because there is such a single-minded focus on the direction of her story.

When revising content, Kaisa is primarily concerned with correctness, not with discovering where the piece can go. She adds words that help match what really happened. Marlow the monkey thought swinging on a vine would be dangerous, but to really fit the situation outlined in the conclusion of her story map, "Don't do things the cool way." Kaisa crossed out her original sentence and rewrote the whole sentence in order to add the word *cool*. Kaisa reads her story only after she has finished writing it. Now she can pause and see what it sounds like. She feels good about it because she knows she successfully took the monkeys through her sequence. And, she happily pictures in her mind the scenes and the colorful details that describe them.

The concern for correctness and convention is demonstrated by Kaisa's ability to correct capital letters and punctuation, especially those ubiquitous exclamation points that find their home in fourth-grade stories. She is also able to circle words of questionable spelling during writing without interrupting her train of thought. Strategies like this, taught in third grade, have become part of her mental process in fourth grade as a result of good teaching and self-accountability. She has an awareness of corrections to be made while she writes and goes back and fixes them when she's done.

At this stage of writing, the care and caution attended to by students provide a safe, clear-cut, and successful base for instruction. Focus and clarity are a by-product of the students' step-by step approach. It is important to begin with what students can do successfully and provide specific teaching structures that will help them move on.

TEACHING ACTIVITY: REVISION STRATEGIES

Written language is far more structured than the spoken word. It is much easier for a student to tell a story using expression, qualification, color, and detail than it is to commit those words to paper. Students often find themselves stranded in the middle of a sentence when they sense elaboration is needed. More than likely the detail is in the mind, but the writer is unable to adequately pause to describe it with a pencil. Thus, the details are sacrificed to keep the thoughts flowing.

When detail or description stand out and make a piece more interesting or exciting, it is worth pointing out.

> His <u>hands were shaking</u> as he grabbed on the vine! He was very scared! He looked down at the ground and he <u>was terrified</u>!

Kaisa made Marlow come to life in this section by using descriptive words and phases that fit the scene.

Note and discuss parts that show good elaboration in your students' writing. Point out specific words that are used effectively. Show students what they've already done well and encourage them to extend that to other parts of their writing. Like Kaisa, most young writers have a linear sense of writing and don't take time to reread. Rereading is important to help them make sense of what they've written. Instruct them to go back and reread sections and specifically show them the way to add, delete, or change important details. Concrete revision strategies, such as the following, become tools for thinking. Model and provide direct instruction for these strategies. What writers do a few times through revision, they do later as a natural means of thinking and rethinking during the process.

Concrete Revision Strategies
- Praise good writing.
- Note good elaboration.
- Have students extend examples of good writing into other writing.
- Point out effective use of words.
- Remind students to reread and make changes to make the writing "sound right."
- Have students add action, dialogue, and sound effects.
- Have students develop appropriate settings for their characters.
- Encourage students to take time to let characters talk to each other.
- Allow characters to weave the plot through dialogue.
- Raise expectations.

Editing Strategies
- Encourage students to reread their writing aloud.
- Remind students to edit for punctuation and uppercase letters.
- Have students circle unknown spelling during writing and go back and correct during revision.

TEACHING ACTIVITY: MICRO-TEXTS IN MINI-LESSONS

It's often a good idea to begin a fourth-grade writing workshop with a 15-minute mini-lesson. Use what students have already written to inform your instruction. By noting what they are already doing, you can make wise choices about what to teach.

Look again at Kaisa's story in Figure 5.1. Although she has done a great job, there are many instructional options for moving her forward as a writer. You could focus on paragraphing, quotations, description, word choice, detail, dialogue, and so on. Decide what it is you need to teach based on group needs, your grade level curriculum, and what will be best for the writer. Keep in mind that learning goes from the known to the unknown. For example, students should be using dialogue in their stories via talk bubbles long before you teach the intricacies of paragraphing and using quotation marks for dialogue. Once the use of dialogue becomes facile, it's easier to teach the mechanics.

Model first by showing—not telling—the writing strategy on which you wish to focus the lesson or series of lessons. Next "hold their hands" as students work with you in a number of possible contexts.

Modeling Writing Strategies

- Write in front of students as you think aloud and construct a piece in your own handwriting.
- Lead a group-dictated language experience story or expository piece to model a feature of effective writing.
- Employ shared or interactive writing in which the teacher and students work together to construct a piece.
- Use student work volunteered by the writer as authentic context.

In each of these instances, the students experience the targeted effective writing practice with your help. Once the concept is firmly in place, volume is important. Do not hesitate to raise the level of expectations by encouraging students to spend more time developing a piece. Students must "practice, practice, practice" what you have taught in the context of their own daily writing.

TEACHING ACTIVITY: LESSON PLANS FOR MINI-LESSONS

Ralph Fletcher, a nationally recognized teacher of writing, recommends taking advantage of "micro-texts"—picture books or skinny books, such as Cheyenne Cisco's 16-page, fully illustrated retelling of the fable, *The Lion and the Mouse*. Micro-texts are often well written, vibrant, eminently readable, and demand little time. This allows the main focus of the lesson to proceed expediently. Micro-texts are good models for writing in grades four, five, and six because they make it easy to show students the text features that you are demonstrating. Micro-texts also work well as teaching tools for writing workshop because, as Fletcher points out, "Reading is up here and writing is down here." But as Fletcher points out, these students can read a fairly complex novel. "Probably the smartest fourth grader in the country cannot write a novel." (Fletcher, 2000)

Micro-texts can be reread often and are useful for following Elizabeth Yates's suggestion of "reading a book like a writer" (Yates, 1995). The lesson will enable students to see and discover the way the author has used his or her craft to make the writing vibrant.

Bring the micro-texts that you really love into your writing workshop. I might use Cheyenne Cisco's *The Lion and the Mouse* in mini-lessons for a variety of purposes.

As a story starter:
"I'm too skinny to eat! Please let me go. Maybe I'll help you one day."

Gentry: Now, let's see how many creative plots we can come up with to finish the story.

To teach synonyms and antonyms:

Bam! The lion's **big/huge**, hairy paw came down on the mouse's **hairy/bald**, pink tail.

Gentry: Cover the bold words. How many words can you think of to go in the blank? Why do you think the author chose the word he did? Use words that have the opposite meanings of the bold words and words that have the same meaning. How do your substitutions change the story?

To teach story organization:

Create a story map for *The Lion and the Mouse*.

To teach dialogue:

One way I might nudge Kaisa forward after she writes the Marlow Monkey story in Figure 5.1 is to show the way dialogue makes a story come alive. First we would read the author's version of *The Lion and the Mouse*. Next we would read it telling what happened but not using dialogue.

Version 1: A big, bossy lion and a quiet, little mouse lived side by side in the jungle.

"Me, myself, and I!" roared the lion. "I'm the best! I'm the boss! I am king of this jungle!"

Version 2: A big, bossy lion and a quiet, little mouse lived side by side in the jungle. The lion roared about being the best and the boss. Oh, was he noisy!

Students are asked to comment on which version they like best and why. Next, as a class or with a student's assistance, we rewrite a scene from a story, such as Kaisa's, adding dialogue. Initially show students how to use talk bubbles for dialogue in their own stories. Then move to more sophisticated dialogue entries.

TEACHING ACTIVITY: MODEL/HOLD THEIR HANDS/ PRACTICE, PRACTICE, PRACTICE

This is a perfect model for virtually everything you teach in reading and writing workshop. I use it here as an example of teaching word choice.

Model first. Once students start using dialogue, they may have a tendency to overuse the word *said*. After reading *When Pigasso Met Mootisse* by

Nina Laden, reread page 12. Model how to avoid the overuse of *said* by replacing all the author's vivid verbs with *said*.

It started one day when Pigasso **said** one of Mootisse's paintings was bad. Then Mootisse **said** one of Pigasso's was bad.

Mootisse **said** Pigasso was an "Art Hog." Then Pigasso **said** Mootisse was a "Mad Cow."

Mootisse **said,** "You paint like a two year old." Pigasso **said,** "you paint like a wild beast."

Mootisse **said,** "Your colors look like mud." Pigasso **said,** "Your paintings look like color-by-numbers!"

Then things really got out of hand.

Hold their hands as students hunt for words to replace *said*. Discuss the dynamics of the scene, emphasizing the characters' feelings during the confrontation. Have students brainstorm vivid verbs to replace *said*. You may wish to show students how to use a thesaurus. Generate a list similar to the following.

yelled	hissed	bellowed	grumbled
screamed	spat	mooed	moaned
hollered	raged	howled	groaned
answered	shouted	shrieked	thundered
questioned	cried	squealed	croaked
called	sobbed	squalled	pouted
wailed	roared	whined	snorted

Ask questions to help students think of unusual words that they might not come up with on their own:

If Pigasso was acting like a snake, he might speak like a snake. What do snakes do? (hiss)
If Pigasso had acted like a mad cat, what might he have done? (spat)
If someone is really, really mad they may be in a _____? (rage)
"Let's turn rage into a past tense verb." (raged)

Continue to hold their hands by working together to rewrite page 12 of *When Pigasso Met Mootisse*, allowing students to discuss word choice and make substitutions for the word *said*. Through discussion, compare the students' version to the author's original version:

It started one day when Pigasso criticized one of Mootisse's paintings. Then Mootisse made fun of one of Pigasso's.

Mootisse called Pigasso an "Art Hog." Then Pigasso **called** Mootisse a "Mad Cow."

Mootisse quipped, "You paint like a two year old. "Pigasso retorted, "You paint like a wild beast."

Mootisse raged, "Your colors look like mud." Pigasso spat, "Your paintings look like color-by-numbers!"

Then things really got out of hand.

Students are now ready to try strategies for making good word choices on their own.

The possibilities for teaching writers in grades four, five, and six are endless. Use some of these suggestions as examples of what you can do. Remember to model, hold their hands, and allow for practice, practice, practice. Then watch your writers soar.

Fourth-grade Writing and Piaget's Stages

Fourth-grade writing is a footprint of how fourth-grade writers think. At fourth grade, writers are likely to be nearing the end of the period and approximate age range for concrete operations—from 7 to 11 years. Initially, their writing still reflects thinking that may be "limited to concrete phenomena and their own past experiences; that is, thinking is not abstract" (Bjorklund, 1995, p. 62).

Writing in concrete operations manifests itself in highly coordinated skills executed concretely in a clear-cut, step-by-step sequence. It is often directed to the objects and events in the fourth grader's immediate experience. The writer often moves determinably through a chain of events or deliberately through a story map, allowing the map to control the piece. Writing may reflect thinking "limited to tangible facts and objects and not to hypotheses" (Bjorklund, 1995, p.82). For example, a fourth grader who is drafting a piece is not likely to shift back and forth during drafting to survey the piece from both perspectives of a reader and a writer; rather, he or she follows a concrete plan from the beginning to the end of the piece. Content in fourth-grade writing generally has referents in real life.

Revision and editing for fourth graders are likely to focus on what is already familiar and what they have previously been taught directly. The focus is on correctness—the correct punctuation, correct spelling, and correct form that have been previously introduced.

As writers in fourth grade gain experience, pieces become longer and more exciting, full of action, dialogue, and even sound effects. Kaisa loves adventure stories and plans her writing with this in mind. She has been taught the value of prewriting and the different forms it can take. She is excited to map out her story and approaches it much like an author might. In the prewriting presented in Figure 5.3 she creates her characters, their personalities, and their relationships.

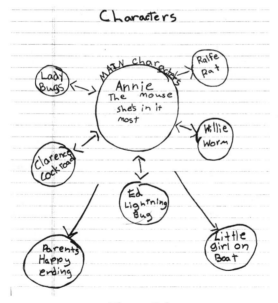

Cockroach - Funny
White Mouse - Know it all
Gray rat - Sea captain
Boy Lady bug - a cook
Girl Lady bug - cute With Bows
Mayfly -
Worm - sees better than anybody
Lightning Bug - always forgets to
turn his Butt off

Characters

Figure 5.3

Next she plans her story in chapters. Chapter 1, "The Decision," demonstrates that she's beginning to control the sequence of events rather than let the story map control her. The chapter format allows her to visit longer with a section and introduce much more content to her reader. She becomes very involved with a sense of putting characters into their setting and is allowing herself to take time to let them talk to each other. Out of this, she unwittingly lets her characters begin to weave her plot through their dialogue. Kaisa's dialogue will come in large chunks and, like most fourth graders, it will be difficult for her to transition back to narrative. Figure 5.4 presents her draft of Chapter 1, "The Decision."

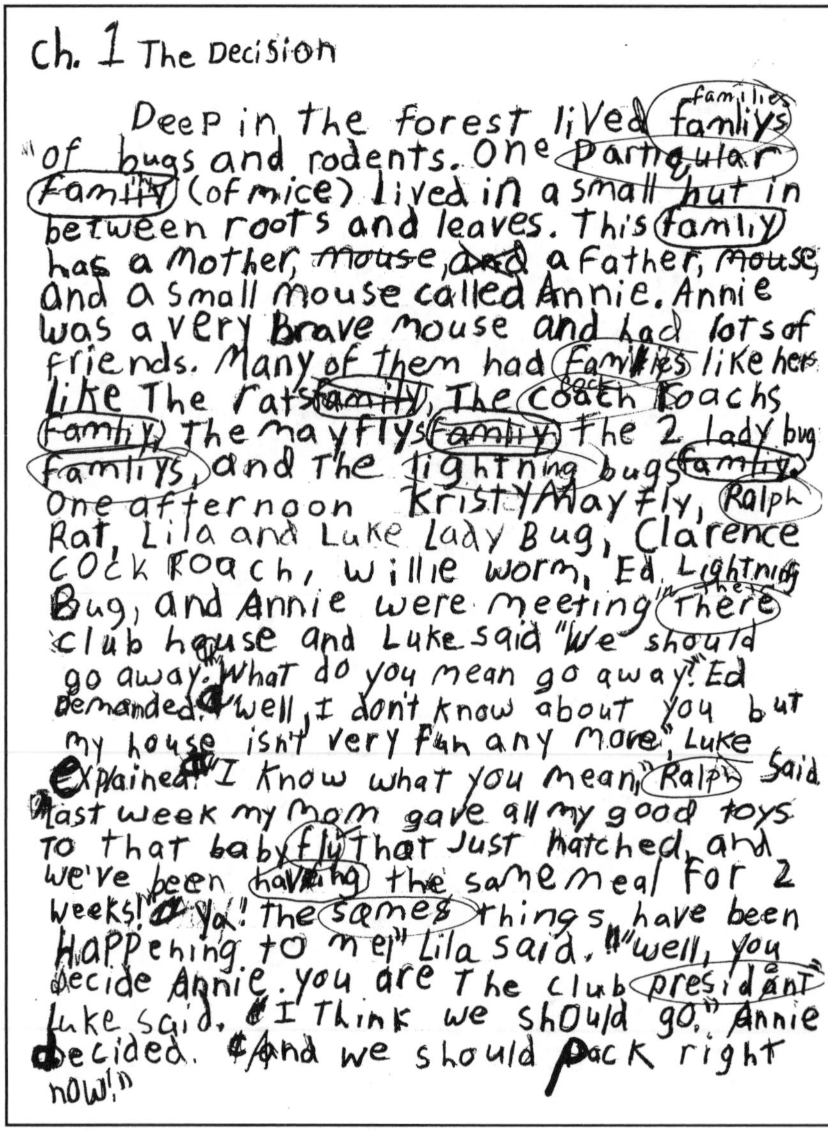

Ch. 1 The Decision

Deep in the forest lived famlys "of bugs and rodents. One particular family (of mice) lived in a small hut in between roots and leaves. This famliy has a mother mouse and a father mouse and a small mouse called Annie. Annie was a very brave mouse and had lots of friends. Many of them had families like hers. like The rats family, The coach roachs famliy the mayflys family the 2 lady bug famliys, and the lightning bugs family. One afternoon Kristy Mayfly, Ralph Rat, Lila and Luke Lady Bug, Clarence Cock Roach, willie worm, Ed Lightning Bug, and Annie were meeting in there club house and Luke said "We should go away." What do you mean go away?" Ed demanded. "well, I don't know about you but my house isn't very fun any more." Luke explained. "I know what you mean." Ralph said "last week my mom gave all my good toys To that baby fly that just hatched and we've been having the same meal for 2 weeks!" "Ya! the sames things have been Happening to me" Lila said. "well, you decide Annie. you are The club presidant" Luke said. "I Think we should go." Annie decided. "And we should pack right now."

Figure 5.4

Kaisa's story will become more involved and exciting for her. As she develops as a writer, she will be able to pause and reread to see how it sounds. The dialogue makes the story easy for her to follow and she's able to move easily back into the writing. Her new ability to think ahead allows her to handle multiple demands in her writing. For example, love grows between two of her characters, and Kaisa's able to plan their wedding while keeping the adventure going.

Kaisa's Transition to Formal Operations

One of the first indications that Kaisa was moving into formal operations at the end of fourth grade was that she began to control the sequence of events in her story rather than let the events of her story map control her. For the first time as a writer, she began to think about her own thinking—to pause as a writer and reread to see how the story sounds. A subplot emerged as she wrote the chapter story that she had not planned for initially—the wedding. Here we see evidence that Kaisa was making the transition into more abstract thinking characterized by formal operations as she examined the content of her own writing, reflected upon the content while drafting, and discovered alternative routes for her story plot.

Kaisa now has the opportunity throughout the course of writing to read some of her story to a small group of peers. In one instance, as she reads aloud, she realizes she has been repetitive with the words *mouse* and *family*. Figure 5.4 shows that she crosses out the words that make her piece sound redundant and unnatural. She wants her writing to sound like her talking and realizes that revising and editing make it possible to reach this objective. Change like this often happens due to internal motivation without teacher prodding.

Kaisa's proofreading and editing shows an awareness of the complexities of using quotation marks. Though inconsistent, she uses the context of her writing to practice what she has learned. She works on the quotations after writing so that the difficulty of the task won't slow her thoughts down. Likewise, she circles unknown spelling words during writing and corrects them later.

Kaisa's story involves a lot of recursive planning, writing, reading, thinking, and talking. It is a most rewarding process for her because of the difficult challenge she placed on herself. The beautiful story and the satisfaction that result make all the hard work of writing worthwhile!

FIFTH GRADE: INDEPENDENCE, FORMAL OPERATIONS, HANDLING THE MULTIPLE DEMANDS OF WRITING

The classroom writing environment has the potential to become a very student-centered place where individuals are free to pursue their own ideas. In fifth grade, friendships are a top priority. These social needs can be fulfilled as students share ideas and talk about writing.

Sarah is Kaisa's best friend. They have many of the same interests and show similar abilities. Their collaboration on stories and narratives provide the motivation to write and help them create effective pieces.

It is important to provide students with a strong sense of the logical stages involved in the process of writing. These stages of prewriting, drafting, revising, editing, and publishing offer a predictable, recursive map that students like Kaisa and Sarah use as a guide. Good models, effective teaching, and plenty of practice help them understand the "whys" and "hows" of each stage. Later writing doesn't reveal what was once a step-by-step process.

For fifth graders the line between the stages in the writing process begins to grow fainter, and there is a growing sophistication about what good writing is. Expository writing provides a clear shift from the stories and narratives of third and fourth grade. Fifth-grade writers are more likely to consider the reader before writing.

Sarah, a fifth grader, has chosen to write about camping with her family. Her prewriting, presented in Figure 5.5, is enjoyable to her because there's so much she wants to tell. She's very thoughtful and organized as she lists the "fun things" and the familiar sequence of activities as she relives the experience. The special details and little adventures surface for Sarah as she shares her adventures aloud with Kaisa. The conversation takes advantage of the social context of writing and serves as a rehearsal as Sarah plans what to share with her reader. As a result, she'll naturally share these details with her reader.

Figure 5.5

When some sort of prewriting is required, students get a sense of direction and maintain focus while they draft. Knowing there is a beginning, middle, and end keeps them on track as they write. Note in Figure 5.6 that Sarah knows her focus ahead of time and allows for the opportunity to elaborate on those "fun things" for her reader.

Camping on An Island

Camping on an island in Maine is one of my favorite things to do. Walking on the beaches, toasting marshmellows and looking for Pirate's Treasure are just a few of the fun things my family and I do!

When we get there the first thing we do is choose a campsite. It's really fun because there're so many different ones. My favorite site is #9 on the harbor side. There's a huge climbing tree and a trail that leads to the rocks and the beach which makes things even more cool. Picking a site may seem dull, but it's really fun! After we put our tent up and go walk on the beach. It's nice to stretch your legs after the long car ride.

There's a log on one of the beaches that my brother, Matty and I play on. I love seeing the sunset from the beach before dinner! I enjoy the beaches on the island. They're really cool!

When it gets dark out after dinner we toast marshmellows. I like mine golden brown, but my dad likes them black (yuck!). It's nice to sit by the fire with a stomach full of marshmellows!

The next morning we get up early and hike on some of the trails. Lots of the trails are loops but some go places, like the trail to Crescent Beach! Sometimes you don't know where you'll end up.

Going on Crescent Beach is fun because I know when I get there it's going to be really cool! There are tide pools with some really cool creatures and seaweed in them! But my favorite thing about it, even though we go in spring or fall, is it is usually warm enough to get a little wet. I always look forward to going there.

Another fun thing to do is to go kayaking. It's really awesome! One time we went out to a couple of islands. It's not hard work and you can explore neat places. Once, before we went kayaking my brother and I found Pirate's treasure! Of course, it wasn't really Pirate treasure, but it was still money! We split it in half.

No matter what you do when you camp on an island, you're bound to have <u>tons</u> of fun!

Figure 5.6

Don't be afraid to take time out to teach about paragraphs. Understanding the value of good paragraph writing becomes a natural part of the process and facilitates fluency of thought. Although students experience paragraph writing in third and fourth grade, they may not gain mastery in writing in paragraphs on their own. Fifth grade is a time to pull this together. Sarah shows how much this knowledge contributes to helping her organize what she wants to say. She understands the concept and function of paragraphs within the context of writing so that topic sentences now help her focus and convey meaning as she writes. In her piece, she consciously underlines the topic sentence (see Figure 5.7) because she knows it will remind her to stay on track.

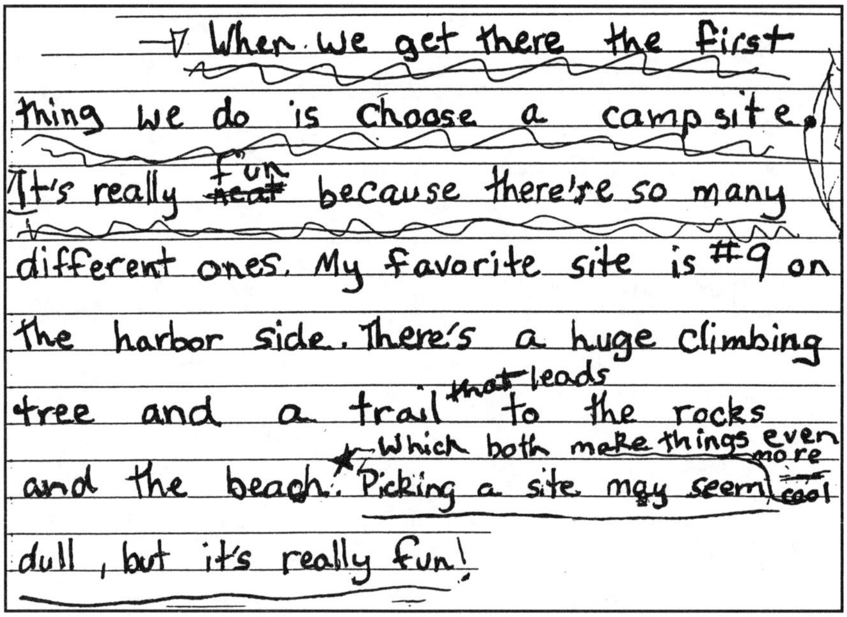

When we get there the first thing we do is choose a campsite. It's really fun ~~neat~~ because there're so many different ones. My favorite site is #9 on the harbor side. There's a huge climbing tree and a trail that leads to the rocks and the beach. Which both make things even more. Picking a site may seem cool dull, but it's really fun!

Figure 5.7

Sarah has learned that separate ideas are explained and expanded upon in paragraphs. The concept of a topic sentence is a strategy that works for Sarah and keeps her focused on the idea. Notice that Sarah crosses out the underlining of the first two sentences and underlines the last sentence as she realizes her topic sentence is not the first one in the paragraph but the last one. She is not thinking about technical paragraph writing but discovers this sentence serves her purpose better. She crosses out her first choice and underlines one that is even better.

TEACHING ACTIVITY: CONNECTING PARAGRAPHS

Turn topic sentences into questions and answer them! Here's a simple process that works very well in helping students build a piece by connecting thoughts in paragraphs. In fifth grade, Sarah successfully uses this process with the two lists presented in Figure 5.8. She begins in List 1 with eight steps in making a bowl on the pottery wheel. In List 2, she turns each of the steps into a question to be answered in a paragraph. Note the way she revises steps 8 and 9 between the lists. Finally, she reconstructs her plan by reorganizing her information into four basic steps written in the left margin of List 2.

List #1

Making a bowl on the pottery wheel is easy once you know how.

~~How~~ is making a bowl easy?
~~once you know how?~~

1 make a ball out of clay
2 slam it on the wheel head
3 turn the wheel on
4 center it by making it flat on top
5 stick your thumbs in the middle and dig down untill you reach ½ in from the bottom
6 pull out the sides
7 shape it the way you want
8 stop the wheel, get it wet and slip a string underneath it and take it off.

List #2

1. How do you make a ball out of clay?
prepare Take a lump of clay and pound it into a ball.
2 How do you slam it on the wheel head?
Take it and put it down hard.
(the wheel head is what you'll be working on)
3 How do you turn the wheel on?
By using the foot pedal.
4 How do you center it?
center Make a right angle with your hands and press down.
5 How do you stick your thumes in?
Put your thumbs together and dig in.
6 How do you pull the sides?
take your thumb and index finger and pull the clay up.
7 How do you shape it?
shape Round it by cupping your hands and shaping the neck.
8 How do you stop the wheel? the foot pedal
9 How do you take it off?
finishing Wet the wheel head and use a piece of wire to slip underneath the bowl and ~~use your~~ carefully lift off.

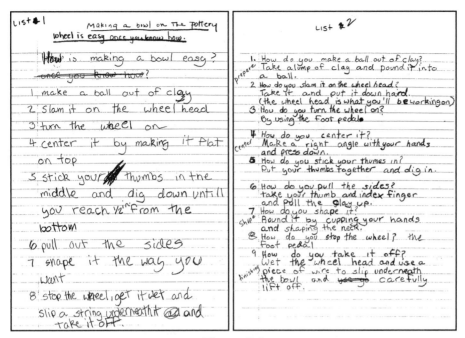

Figure 5.8

Turning her topic sentences into questions and answering them enables Sarah to reflect on her plan. When it came time to write, she knew exactly where she was going as Figure 5.9 demonstrates.

Making a bowl on the pottery wheel is easy once you know how. There are 4 basic steps; preparing the clay, centering, shaping, and adding finishing touches. Preparing the clay. The first step is to take a lump of clay about 3/4 of a pound in weight. Pound it into a ball so when you're centering it will be easier. Don't pound very long though, or the clay will dry out. Then take your ball of clay and drop it on the wheel head (the rotating flat surface of a wheel) and make sure it's secure. Now turn your wheel on, if you are using an electric wheel you can use the foot pedal, if you are using a kick wheel, kick until it's going pretty fast. When you've done this you are ready to start working on the wheel.
Next comes centering. That's when you get the clay to balance out. You'll need to wet you hands alot, so keep a container of water close by. Wet your hands and put your thumbs together holding your other fingers out, forming a right angle. Keep in that position, cup your hands and push down. You'll know it's centered when the top is flat and not wobbling. After you've got it centered, you need to make the hole in the middle. Wet your hands again and put your index fingers together. Now dig down ½ an in. from the bottom. Now you are free to shape and be creative.

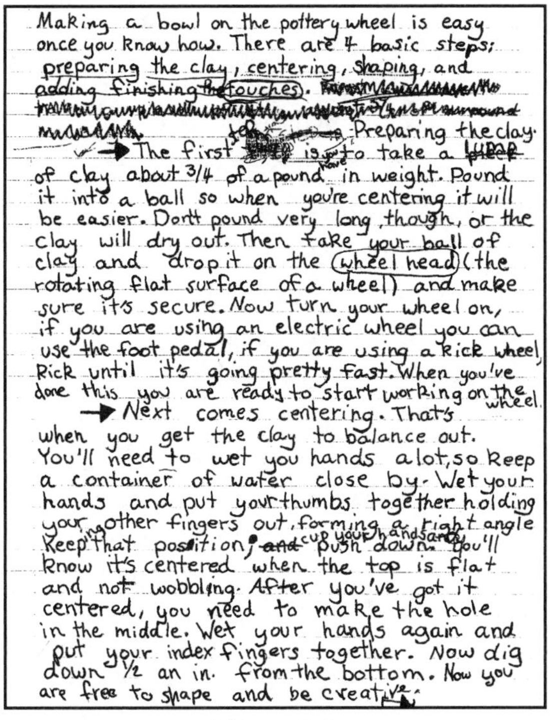

Figure 5.9

What are the results? Planning ahead provides focus, direction, and sequence for Sarah. Turning steps into questions gives her the opportunity to elaborate as she describes the steps effectively. And, using the steps as a guide, she has the ability to turn each into a well-written, informative paragraph. Sarah states: "After all the hard work I knew what I was going to say. I knew that I could refer to the planning and everything was right there. I knew I could actually explain what I was talking about better because once you turn it into a question you have to answer that question. That helps you to explain it. I think I'm a better writer because I used the information and the ideas in my head and it all just melted together when I wrote."

Moving from paragraph to paragraph involves learning about transitioning a reader from one thought to the next. Both Sarah and Kaisa had the opportunity over time to discuss aspects of their writing in which they noticed marked improvement. Some of the transition sentences they found over time in their writing are listed below. Compare these excerpts among different types of writing. Notice the way the transitions move from directly and concretely speaking to their reader to a deeper level of thinking and a more natural flow about a piece of writing.

Transition Statements from Sarah and Kaisa's Writing

- I'm done telling you about my friends, now I'm going to tell you about my family and me.
- I think I've told you everything there is to know about me. I hope you enjoyed this autobiography because I enjoyed writing it! Well, bye!

- The North and South were different in many ways and in this essay you will find out why they were different.
- So now you have learned why the North and South are different.

- Harriet Tubman, the Moses of the people, is an amazing woman.
- Growing up prepared her for this life.

- So, we're left to decide if this man was crazy or if he was a man with a cause that died for his beliefs.
- I strongly urge people to read this book and hope that they will be moved by it as I was.

With time, practice, and help students find it easier to know there are different ways to say the same thing. In the same way that we must help young children move out of invented spelling into standard spelling, we must model specific conventions, such as the awareness of transitions, that will help improve the quality of a piece.

When Kaisa finished a piece on traveling, she was asked to choose a specific area to revise and make better. She chose transitions and pulled out those that in her view, "weren't very good." Here's how she rewrote them.

Original Transitions	Revised Transitions
I love traveling and there are some places I would really like to go to.	I love to travel because I like to see new things in faraway places. There are some fascinating places I would love to go to.
First of all I would just love to go to Egypt.	I've been doing a lot of researching on Egypt and it sounds like a really cool place to go.
I really enjoy seeing California with all the grapevines.	I really enjoy seeing pictures of northern California and all the vineyards. I wouldn't mind visiting there for a long time!

Both Kaisa and Sarah had the opportunity to look at and compare their growth in saying the same thing differently and in using good transitions. When they realized their success, they beamed. "It's easy to flow into the next paragraph. You still have the same train of thought even though you're talking about a different thing. You're still connecting it."

Fifth grade is a time for taking your time. Students take time to plan, to talk, to write and rewrite, to read and reread. And writing reveals fifth graders' capabilities to take time to weigh and to think through their options.

Fifth-grade Writing and Piaget's Stages

Fifth-grade writing is a footprint of how fifth-grade writers think. At fifth grade, writers are likely to be entering the beginning of the period and approximate age range for formal operations—from 11 to 16 years. They are much more likely "to introspect about their own thought processes and, generally, can think abstractly" as writers (Bjorklund, 1995, p. 62). They are no longer tied to concrete objects such as a story map or to the events in their immediate experience. They can think about their own thinking as they write. Instead of being controlled by the story map, for example, the map is much more likely to change as they hypothesize during their writing about what is possible. Writing often reflects deductive reasoning (moving from the general to the specific) that is not limited to what they have experienced but includes new possibilities based on the hypothetical. Writing also reflects inductive reasoning (moving from specific observations to broad generalizations) as in Sarah's writing in Figure 5.8 when she goes from eight concrete events in the making of a bowl on the pottery wheel to four general stages in the process.

Fifth-grade writers often acquire new information as a result of internal reflection. We saw this happen for Sarah as she examined the content of her own thoughts in the writing process. She started out with a list of eight concrete events, and she reflected upon these. Instead of writing a piece with eight paragraphs, she discovered a new way to present her information—preparing the clay, centering, shaping, and finishing—which she presented in four paragraphs. This shift represented an abstraction of her original plan. She discovered an alternative route for presenting her information.

Not only is fifth-grade writing more abstract, but also likely to demonstrate more knowledge about what constitutes good writing and more independent thinking on the part of the writer. Focus during revision and editing is not solely on correctness but on alternatives. Much more internal reflection is likely.

SIXTH GRADE: WRITER'S INTUITION, WRITING IN THE MIND, GOING DOWN DEEP

Many a sixth-grade student can be seen with pencil in hand staring out the window, writing in their minds. The growing understanding about components of the writing process and the conventions that support it help sixth graders develop sophistication about good writing. They can test out ideas with little effort; they experiment and move around their pieces more easily. "Rules" aren't necessary because an intuitive feel for what's good and what isn't surfaces. Writing becomes a channel for thinking as students play with words and ideas.

If we are to teach writing well, the writing voices of students need to be heard. In real life, each student has his or her own unique voice. As a writer, he or she needs to develop a writer's voice. Developing a personal voice on paper, however, requires an early awareness that the words need to be so real that they step right off the page and grab the reader. Sixth-grade students have no problem pretending to be a particular person as they write narratives and are able to use a new voice with each new character. However, when the shift is made into information writing, voice often begins to disappear. What does appear is writing that looks and sounds very much like the encyclopedias and textbooks the words were copied from.

What has happened? Most obviously, students can't write as experts on a subject until they're comfortable with it. The old cliche, one has to write about what one knows, is applicable for sixth-grade students. In order to go deep into a subject and discover voice, they need to experience the knowledge of the subject they're writing about.

In sixth grade, Kaisa and Sarah spent months learning about the Civil War. They were immersed in reading and writing projects, field trips, and interaction with experts. The learning was interesting, powerful, and meaningful. Much of their rich understanding of the Civil War came by way of reading well-written historical fiction and biographies that were replete with voice. When the unit was completed, Kaisa and Sarah chose to work together on a final project. They decided to publish a newspaper on the events surrounding the war and spent time planning, organizing, drafting, and publishing a wonderful piece of writing. It richly demonstrated all of their learning. Because they knew their subject well, they were able to go deep into it. Notice the way voice emerges so naturally in the excerpts in Figure 5.10 from their "Opinion" page:

Dear Editor,
My wife and I strongly believe in slavery. Slaves are just a part of life down south. We don't care if they're people or cattle. They need us to care for them. The south needs the slaves and the slaves need the south. If one falls, then, so does the other. Why, I'm willing to bet 200 sacks of cotton that if the slaves are freed the south will fall apart!

Sincerely,
William Slayer

Slam on Slavery

Before reading "Uncle Tom's Cabin" I would have said that slavery is just something we have to live with. Now I strongly oppose it. Harriet Beecher Stowe's book is truly moving, yet I was shocked to find most of it was true. I had no idea how awful slavery was until I read this book. I held my breath every moment I read it!

Eliza's harrowing escape from slavery changed not only my perspective on slavery but on life. Her plans to escape so that she and her baby could live a better life made the terror of slavery more real.

I strongly urge people to read this book. I hope they will be as moved by it as I was and that their perspective on slavery would be changed or deepened.

Figure 5.10

Kaisa and Sarah are speaking to their readers by tuning into what their articles need to say. They're listening to what they're saying as they write and are thinking about the way their reader will perceive it. Voice happens during a draft—not before or after—and reveals the meaning of the writing as the reader is led into it. Donald Murray says voice establishes the tone of communication between the reader and the writer: "I read the openings I draft over and over listening to the music of the evolving text. Yes, my writing has my voice but, more important, it has its own voice, my voice tuned to the subject, its treatment, its audience" (Murray, 1982).

Voice is one of the most powerful elements in writing. Sometimes it holds the emotion in a piece and speaks quietly through the words. Sarah's beautiful writing in the following journal entry (Figure 5.11) reveals the heart of a Civil War soldier's thoughts:

July 3rd - Gettysburg

As I stood there with all the men standing in a line as far as I could see I thought, "If this is the last time I breathe then so be it." But really even though I put on a good face I couldn't help wondering if I would ever see my home again or taste Ma's quince pie. How I wished I could just disappear right then and there.

I thought back to the first battle in Manassas, how scared I had been and I must admit I thought I'd be brave at a moment like this, like I was at previous battles.

I looked way up at Seminary Ridge where Yankee cannons were pointing down at me. I saw the round tops with more cannons, but most of all I saw the long rolling wheat fields ahead and that was what scared me; not the cannons or the Union soldiers behind the big stone wall. I wondered if the Billy Yanks could see my knees trembling or how my gun quavered in my shaking hands.

I recalled one day, Lee had said, "It is a fine thing war is so horrible for otherwise a man could get to love it." I didn't agree with him then and I still don't now. If we could get to love war, then can't we love peace?

Andrew Tuney
5th Virginia Infantry

Figure 5.11

Voice speaks to the reader throughout the writing; it gives the piece a focus. Sarah wrote without planning ahead and without lengthy pauses. When she finished, she felt tremendous personal satisfaction with what she had written and, in this instance, saw little need to revise.

Kaisa wrote quickly and furiously as she pictured her soldier during "Pickett's Charge" (see Figure 5.12). When she took a breath and went back to reread, she discovered that she had changed verb tenses. The tense change interrupted her own process of trying to hear the voice aloud, and she set out to fix it. Her revising demanded revisiting the scene and required not only correcting tenses but rewording some of the phrases to make them fit. Now, revising for her comes intuitively. It is no longer simply a lockstep part of the writing process, but a process of revisiting all aspects of the content of the piece. For Kaisa, revising is a tool to achieve fluency and cohesiveness in the message she is sending to the reader.

In both pieces, Sarah and Kaisa reveal a sense of the true story of that time of war in our country. Their topics are small but the issue is big, and through the voices of two soldiers they come to understand the horror of war. The process has evolved beautifully over the course of time for these young writers. They don't need to do as much concrete prewriting as they did in earlier grades. Preparation is in the knowing and the thinking. Revising is the writer understanding that the reader wants to make sense of it all. Spelling, grammar, and mechanics become a more natural part of communicating what the writer and the writing hold dear.

"Oh no! Oh no! Oh no!" I feel like I'm shouting it but really I'm just thinking it. Here I am only 15 years old; I'm to young to die. The reason I'm saying that is because General Lee is making us charge over up to the union in an open wheat feild. How dumb is that? I know we're all gonna die, the other soldiers know we're gonna die, so why do it, that's what I'd like to know! But of course I can't ask ~~the general knew.~~ ~~But of course I can't~~ because you never question the general. But if I could I would tell him he has some mind through making us try and shoot ~~behind~~ rocks that the federals are hiding behind.

But then of course it doesn't matter because we're all going to die anyway.

I'm ~~I was~~ thinking I never should have lied about my age in the first place. I heard the person next to me mumbeling something but I can't ~~couldn't~~ make out what it is ~~was~~; he's probably saying what I'm ~~was~~ thinking. ~~Right then and there~~ I heard the loudest cannon fire I've heard in a long time. "Ahhh!" ~~I saw~~ The just person next to me fall. My heart is ~~was~~ beating so fast! ~~I was~~ Lucky that time! More soldiers are going down by the second! ~~I saw another go down.~~ My heart is ~~was~~ beating so fast now I'm sure it will explode! Oh when will this end? Of course it's just begun. The infantry haven't even fired yet. But wait! We're charging. I heard the men all around me yelling. Dozens are going down. No, it must be hundreds! I can't take this anymore! I've been through so many battles but this is the worst! "Fire I'm firing! I'm firing! They're turning around! your gun!" "Fire your gun!" ~~I fired and charged.~~ ~~After a few more fires they~~ ~~started turning around.~~ "What are we doing?" "Retreating to Richmond!"

"We're surrendering?" "No, regrouping." There are hardly any men left to retreat. telling Lee's ~~told~~ Pickett to go back again and fight. Pickett said, "General Lee, I have then no men. ~~When I heard that~~ I knew the "Billy Yanks" had won the battle.

Figure 5.12

When writing is properly taught, it is reasonable to expect students to reach a new level of sophistication around the sixth-grade level. Perhaps Kaisa's and Sarah's revelations of how they felt about their development as writers best describe this achievement:

"Writing is good now. We know what has to happen. We have more experience." (Kaisa)

"Yes, and you know what, I've realized something else. You get smart when you write!" (Sarah)

Not only did they recognize they had reached a level of comfort with writing as a craft, they recognized the powerful impact writing can have in clarifying and changing the way one thinks.

Sixth-grade teachers often ask what changes they should look for in the writing of their students. Here's a list of characteristics of sixth-grade writers to help you assess their writing development:

THINGS DEVELOPING SIXTH-GRADE WRITERS DO

- Write for the reader as they increase volume in information and report writing
- Maintain voice as their writing gains information
- Use prewriting, editing, and revision naturally and recursively
- Show growing sophistication about what good writing is
- View conventions (grammar, spelling, etc.) as a responsibility to communicate well to the reader
- Use conventions of the writing process intuitively
- Use details more effectively
- Use more mental operations while drafting (less trial and error)
- Use writing as a means of clarifying their thinking
- Show the ability to develop some sense of the whole piece before drafting without having to use a concrete story map
- Begin to write with voice more naturally
- Allow their writing voice to lead them
- Bring voice to nonfiction pieces
- Look at a piece through the eyes of the reader
- Reread and revise as they draft
- Allow revisions to be guided by the content of a piece and the way they want their reader to respond
- Weave dialogue in naturally
- Vary beginnings, endings, and transitions

The following teaching activities have been used effectively in sixth-grade writing workshops. Each activity is designed to fit a 15-minute segment of a 45-minute writing workshop. Keep in mind that the mini-lesson is not a one shot deal. The concept presented in a mini-lesson may be taught over a series of weeks or even more extended periods of time. The basic format for the procedure remains the same: model; hold their hands; practice, practice, practice.

TEACHING ACTIVITY: WRITE WITH VOICE

Students often tend to lose voice when they get caught up with trying to write about information they have collected. Sometimes their writing reflects texts and encyclopedias rather than deeper understandings and their own ideas. Kaisa and Sarah had just the opposite experience. They got caught up in the wonderful books they were reading on the Civil War because of the voice of the authors. They developed a sense of being right there during the war. In their Civil War study over a period of several months they neither used history textbooks or encyclopedias. Their own exposure to voice in the literature they were reading was a precursor to the voice they would eventually use in their writing. In sixth grade, as at other levels, the best readers often become the best writers.

Demonstrate voice in writing workshop by sharing wonderful books that reveal voice. Contrast these selections with selections lacking voice. You might read selections on the same topic from an encyclopedia and contrast it to a short selection in a good piece of literature to generate class discussion. Select literature you love to share with your class. Help students analyze the characteristics of voice in these selections.

Model use of voice by sharing student selections in class that demonstrate effective writing with voice. Sharing and class discussions along with concrete models from your students' writing generate motivation, enthusiasm, and new learning. Often students gain confidence in their own abilities as writers when they see examples of successful writing being shared within their own community of writers.

TEACHING ACTIVITY: NARROW THE TOPIC

Topics assigned for reports are often very broad (oceans, space, Civil War, etc.). You may find your students so swamped with information that they don't know where to begin. Powerful writing comes out of small issues that convey a sense of the topic, such as "Pickett's Charge." It is important for teachers to model the way to take a broad subject and narrow it to one manageable aspect of the topic. Sixth graders may run into trouble when a topic is too broad. The focus and direction get lost in writing and the piece goes astray. Show students easy steps for narrowing the topic and staying on track. Figures 5.11 and 5.12 showed Kaisa and Sarah's writing. Here's the process that worked for them and should work for each of your students:

ORIGINAL TOPIC: CIVIL WAR
Step 1: List the possible subtopics of interest to writer.
    Gettysburg

Comparison of Grant and Lee
Appomattox
Stonewall Jackson
Bull Run

Step 2: Choose one topic (Gettysburg) and brainstorm ideas to narrow
the topic a second time.
Chamberlain
Big and Little Round Top
Jeb Stuart's Cavalry
Lee's Mistake
Weapons
Smoke, Dead Guys, Cannons, Blood
Pickett's Charge
Lincoln's Gettysburg Address
Mead

Step 3: Once the topic is chosen (Pickett's Charge), create a simple web
(Figure 5.13) to help the writer visualize the setting and recreate
the scene (from details already in his or her head).

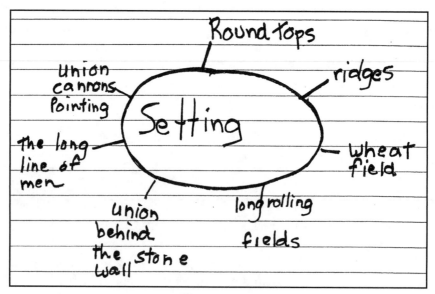

Figure 5.13

Their knowledge allowed them to see Pickett's Charge as a powerful
turning point in the war. Writing from the hearts of soldiers in the midst of
the conflict brought the battle to life for the reader.

TEACHING ACTIVITY: DEMONSTRATE REREADING

Rereading is a powerful practice for sixth-grade writers, but unless it's demonstrated, students don't do it. (Note what happened when Kaisa reread her Pickett's Charge piece in Figure 5.12.) All writers in any situation find some changes are needed when they reread. I have observed the following general sequence as students develop as writers who reread:

Third and fourth graders may not be able to reread while drafting because they often get off track. When they're asked to go back and reread, few changes other than mechanical changes get corrected. Most third and fourth graders aren't effective rereaders.

Fifth graders are more likely to pause and reread but they tend to make specific rather than real complex changes. They make more content-related changes than fourth graders.

Sixth graders can constantly interrupt, reread, rethink, and change as they go. They can plan ahead, think back, alter, add, and change thoughts. They can go back and reread to see how it sounds to the reader.

In planning mini-lessons for your sixth-grade writing workshop, choose instances when you observe a student who is drafting. Ask him or her to reread and make changes such as those described on page 94, teaching word choice, and shown in Figure 5.12. Ask the student to share his or her rereading process as a demonstration in the class writing workshop. On an overhead projector, show the section of the student's writing where the rereading and revising occurred. Model the revising process in a "think aloud," to generate class discussion. In a follow-up mini-lesson, you might choose another student's piece and work through it with the whole group, soliciting students' help in rereading and revising one specific aspect of the piece.

In general, sixth graders don't like to proofread. The secret is to help sixth-grade writers develop a habit of caring for the reader of their writing. Kaisa and Sarah sometimes resisted proofreading and made comments such as "It's icky, boring, not fun and you have to correct it even though you think it's OK." Ultimately they confessed "Proofreading is really for the reader so the reader won't be confused. That's OK."

TEACHING ACTIVITY: USE MODELS FROM GOOD LITERATURE

Many sixth-grade teachers use good literature as springboards for writing or writing study. Students who read a lot have an advantage as writers because the reading and writing processes share many of the same knowledge sources. Integrating aspects of reading and writing workshop is a very efficient use of time. *The Great Fire* by Jim Murphy is a piece of literature that might be used to model "eyewitness accounts" in reading workshop and as a springboard for writing "eyewitness accounts" in writing workshop.

Sixth-grade Writing and Piaget's Stages

At sixth grade, writers continue to demonstrate abstract thinking and increased ability to examine the contents of their own thinking as writers. Their formal operational skills increase. They are older, cognitively more advanced, and no longer in a transition phase between concrete and formal operations. They assimilate information into abstract schemes, test their own hypotheses as writers, question their own thinking while writing, and demonstrate reflective abstraction in their writing with ease.

The sixth-grade writer not only demonstrates more abstraction as a writer but also continues to demonstrate even more knowledge about what constitutes good writing and more independent thinking.

Writing is one of the most significant areas of potential growth for fourth-, fifth-, and sixth-grade students. "Footprints" of students' thinking are clearly left behind in their writing. You can even monitor evidence of the move from concrete to more abstract thinking by watching what each student does as a writer. Observing writing helps you know the student, and teaching writing effectively opens up him or her to new avenues of thinking. When you observe what students do as writers and offer models and guidance, they reach new levels of craft as writers and new levels of sophistication as thinkers.

Remember these goals for writers by the end of sixth grade. Much of the preparation for writing will be in the knowing and the thinking for both the craft and the topic. Revising occurs when the writer understands that the reader wants to make sense of the piece. Spelling, grammar, and mechanics largely become a natural part of communicating what the writer and the writing hold dear.

Ultimately, your goal as a teacher is to help your students reach levels of competence and confidence so that they come to a realization similar to Kaisa and Sarah's: "Writing is good now. We know what has to happen. You get smart when you write."

CHAPTER 6

TEACHING VOCABULARY IN GRADES FOUR, FIVE, AND SIX

By Margaret Trauernicht

"So many things have gone out of date. But after all these years, words are still important. Words are still needed by everyone. Words are used to think with, to write with, to dream with, to hope and pray with."

From *Frindle* by Andrew Clements (1996)

Author's note: *Through Andrew Clements' character, Mrs. Lorelei Granger, fifth-grade teacher, we learn the significance of the power of words and the importance of teaching them. In this chapter, I've invited Margaret Trauernicht, a master classroom teacher, instructor of language arts and children's literature at the University of Nebraska-Omaha, educational consultant, and expert on vocabulary instruction to share her insights on teaching vocabulary in grades four, five, and six. Teaching words amounts to teaching students to think. An ideal time for children to discover the power of words is in grades four, five, and six.*

Traditionally, fourth-, fifth-, and sixth-grade teachers have devoted time to teaching vocabulary. There is a growing research base for this practice. For example, a comprehensive analysis of research studies in the *Report of the National Reading Panel: Reports of the Subgroups* (2000, pp. 4-33) supports vocabulary instruction and lists important teaching implications including:

- Vocabulary instruction should be taught both directly and indirectly.
- Repetition and multiple exposures to vocabulary in authentic contexts are important.
- Learning in rich contexts is valuable for vocabulary learning.

- Vocabulary learning should entail active engagement in learning.
- Dependence on a single vocabulary instruction method will not result in optimal learning.

There seems to be little doubt that you should teach vocabulary in grades four, five, and six. Perhaps the biggest challenge is to decide how to match each student with words that are just right for him or her. It's impractical to discuss every word that might be unfamiliar to your students. Too often, fourth-, fifth-, and sixth-grade teachers tend to try to cover too many words and end up teaching them superficially. Avoid this pitfall by choosing fewer words to teach in depth.

Your students' interests are critical in considering which words to highlight in vocabulary study. The words children need to learn will also vary greatly depending upon their experiences, reading levels, and volume of reading. Guidelines to help you choose include:

- High-utility words
- Words that connect to other curricular areas
- Words from your course of study
- High-interest words
- Some student choice words

This chapter includes six engaging activities for teaching vocabulary in grades four, five, and six. [Examples of how to use the activities with a fourth-grade selection, *Shiloh,* by Phyllis Reynolds Naylor and a sixth-grade selection, *Roll of Thunder, Hear My Cry,* by Mildred D. Taylor are provided in the Appendix.] All six activities meet the requirements of multidimensional reading programs as well as the needs of individual students. These activities carry out research-based implications, such as findings in the McKeown, Beck, Omanson, and Pople's study (1985):

> "...4th graders performed well with instruction that extended beyond single class periods and involved multiple exposures in authentic contexts. The instruction added activities to extend use of learned words beyond the classroom and high-frequency encounters with words."
>
> From the *Report of the National Reading Panel: Reports of the Subgroups* (2000, pp. 4-22)

To illustrate each activity, I've chosen *Mrs. Frisby and the Rats of NIMH* by Robert C. O'Brien, a fifth-grade literature selection.

Mrs. Frisby and the Rats of NIMH, like most of the literature you choose, provides a variety of interesting and challenging vocabulary words for your students. I've included about one-third of the words I consider good choices for fifth-grade study. It's impossible to study them all and still have time for the most important activity—reading. Vary the teaching activities you use. You might think it would be impossible to do all six activities described below, but all were completed within a three-week reading of the book in my classroom. Actively engage students in discussing, role-playing, categorizing, or drawing illustrations of words rather than copying dictionary definitions or completing worksheets. Offer a variety of activities that are social and meaningful. The hands-on nature of the activities eliminates perceptions of vocabulary study as busywork. Additionally, the activities help students realize that retention and application of the words in their speaking and writing goes beyond the study of the novel.

TEACHING ACTIVITY: CONTEXTUAL ANALYSIS

In this activity you will show your students how to analyze the text in which a word is presented to find an explicit or implied meaning of a targeted word. Using context clues embedded in authentic text is not only supported by research (*Report of the National Reading Panel: Reports of the Subgroups*, 2000, pp. 4-33), it's practical because readers encounter most new words in context. Conduct whole-class and small-group vocabulary sharing sessions to generate interest in words, to model how to use context cues, and to form vocabulary-building consciousness. Give students some choice in which words to inspect. Routinely ask, "What do you think the word means in that sentence? Make an educated guess. What contextual evidence supports your definition?" Ideas for contextual analysis and discussions are presented for *Mrs. Frisby and the Rats of NIMH*.

The teaching hints that follow should be presented as quiet comments, leading questions, or reflective thinking—not as didactic statements. Allow students to do the thinking rather than give them the answers. Introduce the teaching hints using questions such as:

Here's a teaching hint. I wonder how it might help?
Why do you suppose...?
How does this hint help you figure it out?

---

fare (p. 3) "There was plenty of food for breakfast and lunch and dinner, too, for that matter; but still the sight depressed her, for it was the same tiresome *fare* they had been eating every day, every meal, for the past month."

Teaching Hint: Simply pointing out the clue words food, eating, and meal should help a student infer the meaning and distinguish it from *fare*, meaning a fee.

---

frailest (p. 8) "But he was also the *frailest*, and when colds or flu or virus infections came around he was the first to catch them and the slowest to recover."

Teaching Hint: Timothy is described as the *frailest* of Mrs. Frisby's children. Help students infer that he is sickly and fragile because he catches infections easily and doesn't recover quickly.

authoritative (p. 23) "'Don't argue. I have only a few minutes.' She said this in a voice so *authoritative* that the crow fluttered down immediately."

Teaching Hint: The context shows that *authoritative* describes Mrs. Frisby's voice. Since the crow did what he was ordered to do right away, help students understand that the voice must have been intimidating. Ask students to tell you how a parent or teacher would say, "Don't argue." Mention that the word *authoritative* comes from *authority* and discuss the way someone in that capacity would give an order.

literally (p. 25) "'I'll drop you off there.' He banked alarmingly and for a moment Mrs. Frisby thought he meant it *literally*. But a few seconds later . . . they were gliding to earth a yard from her front door."

Teaching Hint: Explain to students when Jeremy the crow tells Mrs. Frisby he'll drop her off, she's afraid he means exactly, or word for word, what he says. The next sentence should help students realize "I'll drop you off there" is a figure of speech—he doesn't really intend to drop her. To understand the word *literally*, compare it to *figuratively*, sharing examples: *If someone say "I'm in hot water" or "I have butterflies in my stomach" or "I've opened up a can of worms" are they speaking literally or figuratively?*

broad (p. 50) "'But the limb is *broad*. You'll be safe enough.' And indeed the limb was almost as wide as a sidewalk."

Teaching Hint: The previous paragraph tells that Mrs. Frisby has landed on a branch of the tree where the owl lives and is worried about the height. Ask students to tell what type of branch would make Mrs. Frisby nervous. Compare things that would be considered either broad or narrow— a path, river, or tunnel—to help distinguish the difference.

sentry (p. 58) "Go there. You will find a *sentry* guarding the door."

Teaching Hint: From the sentence it's easy to infer that a *sentry* is someone who guards a door. Students might have heard the word in regard to a military person. Have students give other examples of where they have seen or heard of sentries.

mutation (p. 123) "We have a real breakthrough, and since it is DNA, we may very well have a true *mutation*, a brand new species of rat.

Teaching Hint: The meaning of *mutation* is explicitly stated after the word: a brand new species. Explore the word further if you have or will study plant or animal mutations in your science classes. Due to ongoing progress made in DNA studies and genetic coding, this word will continue to be heard and read in the news.

toiling (p. 167) "They entered the bins, took off their harness sacks, filled the sacks with grain, put them on again, and left through the tunnel, out the back door. They looked, Mrs. Frisby thought, like very large ants endlessly *toiling* on an anthill."

Teaching Hint: Three clues are given in context that will help students: The rats are keeping very busy gathering grain, which is hard work; They are doing it endlessly, which means without resting; Ants are known to be hard workers.

TEACHING ACTIVITY: ACTING OUT WORDS

There are a large number of words in *Mrs. Frisby and the Rats of NIMH* that could best be taught by students acting out words or role-playing a situation to demonstrate a word's meaning. This activity allows students to form an association and remember the context that accompanied the word as well as its meaning. Acting out words works well with verbs but can also be effective with other parts of speech.

warily (p. 3) "She climbed up the tunnel, emerging whiskers first, and looked around *warily*."

The word describes the way Mrs. Frisby pokes her head out of the tunnel hole above the ground. Volunteers could act this out. Have students suggest other situations when someone would act warily, such as students walking home and encountering a strange dog or withdrawing money at an automatic bank teller's window late at night with someone suspicious nearby. Have students think of other times they are on guard or cautious about something. Remind them that warily is an adverb, describing the way something is done.

hypochondriac (p. 9) "He was also–perhaps as a result–something of a *hypochondriac*."

Have a student role-play a scene as if he or she is a hypochondriac. By the time the student has completed telling about all his or her physical illnesses, everyone should have a better understanding of the word.

scurry (p. 12) "Always she kept an eye out for hiding places–logs, roots, stones, things to *scurry* under if she should meet a larger animal who might be unfriendly."

Emphasize that this is a type of movement made by small, quick, darting creatures that is usually done quietly. Discuss animals that might scurry. It might be helpful to stress that *scurry* rhymes with *hurry* and if you don't scurry you're moving slowly. Students will enjoy acting out this word.

cordial (p. 73) "'Why, so it is Mrs. Frisby. How do you do?' He sounded *cordial* enough, but he was startled."

Have a student role-play a scene where he or she meets someone who is cordial. Then have the same student or another role-play someone who is not cordial. Brainstorm words that describe each type of person. Also name cordial persons, such as the school secretary, school nurse, or a particularly friendly person that your students know. It is helpful to connect a person or character to an adjective.

baffled (p. 96) "Mrs. Frisby, looking at their *baffled* faces, felt her delight subsiding."

Role-play someone who is baffled (scratches head, says, "huh?" or "I don't get this!") Discuss things that baffle students, such as math problems, the solution to a puzzle, magic tricks, unsolved mysteries, and so on.

cowered (p. 115) "I *cowered* to the back of the cage, which was just what he expected me to do."

Emphasize that someone cowers because of fear or shame. Have students pretend to be Mrs. Frisby in the cage. Other examples of cowering might be acted out, such as a small, helpless creature cornered by a predator.

reluctantly (p. 141) "Finally, *reluctantly*, everyone agreed to spend one more day in the laboratory and leave early the next night."

Ask students what they do reluctantly—their homework, clean their rooms, or get up in the morning. Encourage students to role-play any of their ideas.

beckoned (p. 166) "He opened a door and *beckoned* her through it."

This is easy to act out. Be sure to emphasize that beckoning is not just calling someone, but involves using hand or head movements as a signal.

pessimist (p. 187) "And he was a *pessimist*. He never believed that we could really make it on our own."

Discuss specific examples from the text, which characterize Jenner as a pessimist. Role-play a typical day in the life of a pessimist from waking up in the morning expecting it to be raining, to knowing there will be no milk for breakfast, to thinking there will be no clean clothes to wear to school, etc. Every student will probably know someone who would fit this description.

retreated (p. 201) "She could watch them, looking down; but if she *retreated* to the far side of the cage, they could not see her, nor she them."

Discuss the way the word was used in the book and how Mrs. Frisby looked when she retreated. Act out the word and describe ways this word is commonly used, such as in war or any kind of fighting, or any time a person needs to get away, just to be alone.

deposited (p. 213) "Behind them they had *deposited* a jumble of equipment . . ."

In the text, the rats deposited a jumble of equipment. It's easy to act out this definition. Set something down on a table and announce, "I just deposited [names of items] on the table." Brainstorm with students other ways the word *deposited* can be used, such as dirty clothes deposited in the hamper, dirt deposited at a construction site, and so on.

TEACHING ACTIVITY: ROOT WORD OR AFFIX ANALYSIS

Learning the meanings of common roots, prefixes, and suffixes as well as word origins are effective tools in unlocking the meaning of new words (Ryder and Graves, 1994). I look for as many opportunities as possible to study word parts in unknown vocabulary. Studying root words, prefixes, and suffixes in a systematic, organized way helps students realize rapid vocabulary growth. *Mrs. Frisby and the Rats of NIMH* provides numerous opportunities to apply knowledge of word parts.

Teach prefixes which mean *not*. Chart the prefixes and have students add words they find in their reading materials, including content reading, to the list.

IM (p. 20) impatient—not patient, (p. 111) impossible—not possible
IR (p. 90) irrelevantly—not relevantly
IN (p. 21) ineffectively—not effectively
DIS (p. 97) disinterested—not interested
UN (p. 96) unlock—not lock
IL (p. 32) illogical—not logical

Identifying a word's base word often helps students understand the target word. Make sure students read the sentence from the text that contains each word. Discuss its part of speech and its use in the sentence. Often, a student will have an understanding of the meaning but use it incorrectly in context.

Page	Word	Base
3	laboriously	labor
34	existence	exist
58	secrecy	secret
60	secretive	secret
116	captivity	captive
170	descendants	descend
185	descended	descend
212	urgency	urge
212	admiration	admire
217	precision	precise
221	tension	tense

Encourage students to come up with words derived from the same base word. For example, if you targeted *admiration*, you might also target *admirable*, another word derived from *admire*. Working with derived forms offers many opportunities to reinforce word parts that are important to vocabulary learning. Another strategy is to offer sentences to students with opportunities to choose the correct form of the word. For example:
a. My mother called with (urgent/urgency) in her voice.
b. The (precise/precision) of the marching band impressed me.
c. Parents are usually (secretive/secrecy) right before a big holiday.
d. My (descent/descended) into the deep hole caused me anxiety.
e. Many scientists question whether aliens really (exist/existence).

Have students create their own sentences to share with the class:

Two words in *Mrs. Frisby and the Rats of NIMH* contain the prefix *fore*: *foresee* (p. 138) and *forewarned* (p. 147). Discuss its meaning, generating a list of other words with the prefix: *forecast, foreshadow, foretell, forefather, foregone, foresight,* and *foreboding.* Comparisons could be made with other words in the text, such as *foreleg* and *forepaw,* which have a slightly different meaning but could be related to and discussed with the other words.

Two words include the root *extend*: *extension* (p. 178) and *extending* (p. 181). Discuss that *extend* means to lengthen or stretch out. In the text, *extension* refers to a cord that needed to be lengthened and *extending* refers to meetings stretching over, going beyond a year. Ask students to think of other instances where they have heard a form of the word *extend*: extend your hand to someone, extend a warranty, extend a subscription, extension ladders, and so on.

The word *semi-circle* (p. 213) describes how the rats stood. The prefix *semi* means half or partly and is used in many words. Have students brainstorm examples and write them on a chart. Encourage students to search for other examples in their reading to add to the chart, such as *semiconscious, semiannual, semi-trailer, semicolon, semiprecious, semiconductor,* and *semi-professional.*

TEACHING ACTIVITY: VISUAL REPRESENTATION

Having students represent a word visually through a drawing allows for more concrete learning. It also provides a creative outlet for the student who enjoys art. Drawing and sketching works best with nouns but can also be used with other parts of speech.

Students may visually represent new words by drawing a picture, bringing in photos from books or magazines, or creating a drawing from the letters in the word. Bringing the word to a more concrete level is always helpful. Use the following words from *Mrs. Frisby and the Rats of NIMH*:

talons (p. 52) "Each of his [the owl's] feathery feet was tipped with five gleaming *talons* an inch long."

stalagmites (p. 53) "It was not really a floor at all but only the jagged ends of dead wood sticking up from below, like *stalagmites* in a cave."

radiated (p. 82) "The room before her was at least three times as big as the one they had just left, and corridors *radiated* from it in as many directions as petals from a daisy."

silos (p. 152) "In the country there were barns and *silos* stocked with grain and corn, and chicken houses full of eggs."

fork (p. 163) "They went on until they came to a *fork* in the tunnel."

foundation (p. 194) "There was a basement under the main part of the Fitzgibbon's house, but the big kitchen had been added later and stood on a *foundation* of concrete blocks."

TEACHING ACTIVITY: SEMANTIC MAPPING

Students learn new vocabulary by categorizing unknown words under familiar topics with other known words (Levin, Levin, Glassman, and Nordwall, 1992). Words with similar characteristics can be learned more effectively if students think about connecting unfamiliar words with words they already know. Have students group words into semantic clusters. For example, the words *palace, shack, trailer, house,* and *teepee* may all be placed in one semantic cluster. While these words are not synonyms, they are related in meaning because they are all residences. One source I've found helpful in teaching vocabulary is Robert J. Marzano's *Literacy Plus Teacher Reference Book to Words in Semantic Clusters*. This resource text includes 12,409 words appropriate for students in grades K-12 and organized into 61 semantic clusters. Marzano chose words students are likely to encounter in reading basals, children's literature, content reading, and standardized tests. Here's what a semantic cluster looks like:

A Semantic Cluster

governor	congresswoman	councilman	delegate
mayor	senator	councilwoman	tribune
congressman	candidate	politician	incumbent

(Marzano, Paynter, Kendall, Pickering, and Marzano, 1991, p. 39)

All of the words above refer to individuals in power who are elected or appointed.

Seeing words organized by shared aspects of meaning helps students make sense of all the words they are trying to assimilate. When students can compartmentalize words in categories, they are developing schema and building word banks in their brains. It is helpful if new words can be given a category label and taught with other words that have similar characteristics. This practice allows students to go from the known to the unknown; they connect an unknown or unfamiliar word to words that are already in their vocabulary. Discussing how the new word is similar to, but also slightly different from, the known word helps to solidify the understanding.

It is also very helpful to have each student keep a vocabulary book divided into categories or semantic clusters. Place each newly learned word in the book in clusters with other words with similar characteristics. Have students create a "Show-you-know"—a drawing, a synonym, a phrase, a specific contextual sentence, or examples of the word—beside each word. The student demonstrates that he or she understands the word's meaning through the "Show-you-know." Figure 6.1 depicts a "Show-you-know."

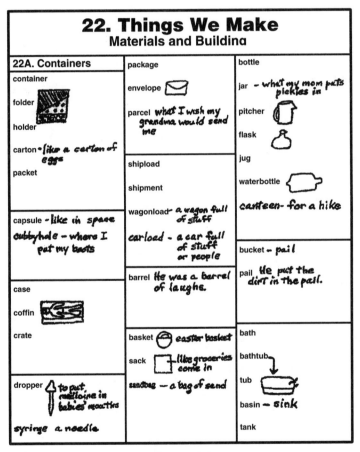

Figure 6.1

Introduce the concept of semantic mapping by modeling or work with students interactively to put words in clusters. Have students discuss similarities and differences among the words. Help students recognize that placing words in categories leads to better understanding.

Try this: Put several cluster headings on chart paper. As the text is read, ask students to consider words in the literature that would be categorized under the following clusters. Discuss each word as it is added to the chart to be sure students understand what each word means and why it is in a particular category.

[**Note:** Numbers preceding cluster headings correspond to super-clusters in *Literacy Plus Teacher Reference Book to Words in Semantic Clusters*. Page references correspond to words in *Mrs. Frisby and the Rats of NIMH.*

37—Diseases/Health
pain (p. 5)
cold (p. 8)
pulse (p. 8)
dizzy (p. 8)
flu (p. 9)
virus (p. 9)
infections (p. 9)
fever (p. 9)

11—Transportation/Work-Related Vehicles
harrow (p. 243)
bulldozer (p. 230)
combine (p. 230)

8—Machines/Engines/Tools
lathes (p. 164)
circular saws (p. 164)
drills (p. 164)
soldering irons (p. 177)
vises (p. 177)
wrenches (p. 177)

12—Mental Actions/Thinking
delirious (p. 10)
paralyzed (p. 14)
bewilderment (p. 58)
astonished (p. 76)
consternation (p. 142)
baffled (p. 154)

5—Feelings/Attitudes
agitated (p. 56)
hostile (p. 83)
indignantly (p. 205)

53—Images/Perceptions/Looking Actions
perceive (p. 50)
detect (p. 126)
distinguish (p. 141)
gaped (p. 164)

Place words either in a binder, divided by clusters, or on note cards to be organized in a file box. Encourage students to decide on the appropriate cluster for the word and other words that would also be in that category. Encourage critical thinking and the possibility that a word might be categorized in different ways. Knowing other words in the cluster will help attach meaning to the new word. Don't tell students the answers! In the following example, I used *Literacy Plus Teacher Reference Book to Words in Semantic Clusters* as an easy reference for additional words and categories.

[**Note about Cluster/Mini-cluster column:** Numbers represent clusters; letters represent subordinate mini-clusters.]

WORD	PAGE	CLUSTER/MINI-CLUSTER	OTHER WORDS
plummeted	41	2–Going, Moving, Stopping P–Descending Motion	tumble, collapse, descend, plunge, topple
expedition	46	2–Going, Moving, Stopping G–Coming/GoingActions Involving Coming/Going	trip, travel, journey, voyage, exploration, excursion, trek
timidly	52	13–Human Traits/Behavior L–Shyness	shy, skittish, bashful, meek, docile, reticent
sympathetically	42	13–Human Traits/Behavior A–Kindness/Goodness	sensitive, understanding, thoughtful, considerate
efficient	93	13–Human Traits/Behavior B–Eagerness/Dependability	productive, effective, industrious, thorough, dependable, responsible, diligent
reluctant	179	13–Human Traits/Behavior P–Caution	cautious, wary, careful, suspicious, watchful, averse
oppose	191	10–Communication B–Confrontation/ Negative Information	reject, decline, rebel, revolt, defy, object, protest, challenge, disagree
notifying	175	10–Communication C–General Presentation of Inform.	tell, describe, present, inform, recount, relate, apprise, convey

WORD	PAGE	CLUSTER/MINI-CLUSTER	OTHER WORDS
convince	201	10–Communication E–Persuasion	influence, sway, lure, persuade, urge, coax, convert
request	58	10–Communication F–Questions	ask, invite, offer, question, propose
scrutiny	94	12–Mental Actions/ Thinking C–Mental Exploration	examination, investigation, experimentation, probe, analysis, inspection
assumed	135	12–Mental Actions/ Thinking D–Mental Actions Involving Conclusions	guess, suppose, estimate, forecast, suspect, predict, infer, conclude, deduce
engrossed	158	12–Mental Actions/ Thinking F–Interest	interested, intrigued, entranced, attentive, curious
astute	138	12–Mental Actions/ Thinking K–Intelligence	adept, aware, clever, capable, wise, shrewd, curious, practical, logical
occasionally	125	7–Time K–Duration/Frequency	sometimes, infrequently, irregularly, periodically, rarely, sporadic
permanently	168	7–Time K–Duration/Frequency	forever, constant, everlasting, continuous, eternal, perpetual, always
preceding	2	7–Time G–Prior Action	earlier, former, already, prior to, before, antecedent, precursor

TEACHING ACTIVITY: CLUSTER CONCENTRATION

Using index cards, play "Cluster Concentration," in which students must match the word to its cluster topic or phrase. One set of cards will have vocabulary words in sentences from the text. The other set of cards will have a category or cluster phrase. The cards are placed face down on a table. Students take turns choosing a card and finding its matching category. If the first two cards selected don't match, the next player takes a turn. When a match is found, the player gets another turn. The student with the most matches wins.

Clusters
Names Indicating Friendship
Filth/Uncleanliness
Containers
Size/Quantity/Amount
Looking Actions
Places for Learning/Experimentation
Money Related to Characteristics
Jewels/Rocks
Weather/Natural Catastrophes
Temperature/Fire
Family Relationships
Parts of Dwellings/Buildings
Actions Done to Soil/Crops
General Upset
Actions Related to Clothing
Lack of Motion

Words in Context Sentences
(p. 62) By the time they reached the garden, it had gone almost completely dark, and Jeremy could not *linger*.

(p. 80) They continued along the *corridor*, which curved always slightly to the right, so Mrs. Frisby could never really tell how long it was.

(p. 83) They did not look hostile, nor were they alarmed—since her two *companions* were familiar to them.

(p. 83) He carried a *satchel—rather* like a handbag—by a strap over his shoulders.

(p. 110) "What's a lab?" "A *laboratory*." "Yes, but what is it?" "I don't know but I think that's where we're going."

(p. 112) The man with the gloves and the boots then *donned* a wire face-mask as well, and climbed in among us.

(p. 50) As they came closer, she could dimly *perceive* a shape like a squat vase sitting in the hollow of the tree.

(p. 22) The size of the brain is no measure of its *capacity*.

(p. 170) Their *descendants* today are the rats known as prairie dogs.

(p. 179) Deep underground, our home stayed warm in winter and cool in summer. It was a comfortable, almost *luxurious* existence.

(p. 188) We've got seeds; we have our plows; we've cleared and *cultivated* part of the land near the pond.

(p. 188) We've even dug some irrigation ditches in case there's a *drought*.

(p. 138) If anyone ever finds the cave, there won't be any evidence of what we've been doing—nothing but broken bits of metal, *debris* that will look like ordinary junk.

(p. 108) And yet you could hardly even call it stealing—it was waste food, and all they did with it was haul it away to the city *incinerator*.

(p. 190) Yet if it was *distressing* to him—he thought—how much more it would be to you!

(p. 246) They didn't plow the particular spot in the garden where we live. It's behind a *boulder*.

(Answers to Cluster Concentration)	
linger	Lack of Motion
corridor	Parts of Dwellings/Buildings
companions	Names Indicating Friendship
satchel	Containers
laboratory	Places for Learning/Experimentation
donned	Actions Related to Clothing
perceive	Looking Actions
capacity	Size/Quantity/Amount
descendants	Family Relationships
luxurious	Characteristics Related to Money
cultivated	Actions Done to Soil/Crops
drought	Weather/Natural Catastrophes
debris	Filth/Uncleanliness
incinerator	Temperature/Fire
distressing	General Upset
boulder	Jewels/Rocks

ACCESSING VOCABULARY LEVELS

You may wish to assess your students' learning of the vocabulary you have targeted in class. Rather than matching or fill-in-the-blank tests, I prefer that students complete "Show-you-knows" for the words. They can write a definition, phrase, original sentence using the word, or draw a specific picture. The sentence must be clear and detailed. For example, a student writing, "I am a pessimist" or "I saw talons" would not earn credit because the sentences are vague, providing no assurance that the student understands the words. On the other hand, "I am a pessimist because I always think my team is going to lose" or "I saw the eagle's sharp talons grab the fish" give an indication that the student understands the words and also uses them correctly in writing. Students need to be trained to learn how to write sentences with adequate information. They need to be taught to evaluate their own "Show-you-knows" as well as those of classmates to become more proficient in writing. Practice in vocabulary improves writing across the curriculum because students learn to become explicit in saying what they mean.

Overall assessment of vocabulary growth based on grade-level benchmarks is problematic because it is difficult to designate grade-levels to words. Assigning grade levels to words based on word frequency doesn't work well because frequency levels change based on the material or literature selections to which the student is exposed. However, some standardized tests, such as The California Achievement Tests (CAT), The Comprehensive Test of Basic Skills (CTBS), Science Research Associates (SRA) Survey of Basic Skills Objectives, or The Stanford Achievement Tests do provide a measure of vocabulary growth.

Another measure is informal assessment by observing vocabulary use in student writing. Look for evidence of vocabulary growth by taking three samples of writing three times a year—at the beginning, middle, and end—and comparing the use of vocabulary in the nine samples. Expect word choices to vary, depending upon the topic or genre. While this type of assessment is very informal, it will give an indication of the student's vocabulary capacity and growth.

The dictionary and thesaurus should become companions for finding and verifying words, not sources for copying definitions. Social interaction, discussion, and application to the students' lives, fewer worksheets, and less memorization are keys to successful vocabulary learning. Students should be held accountable for the words studied.

VOCABULARY ASSESSMENT CHECKLIST

Does the student:
1. Use context clues to understand new vocabulary?
2. Have knowledge of basic semantics and use word parts such as prefixes, suffixes, and roots to unlock the meaning of unknown words?
3. Act out new words to help solidify their meanings?
4. Use new vocabulary in his or her writing?

5. Edit his or her writing for word choice, choosing more specific and interesting words?

6. Graphically represent a word in a sketch or drawing or bring in an example or photo to demonstrate understanding of new vocabulary?

7. Use reference materials such as the dictionary, glossary, and thesaurus?

8. Keep a vocabulary journal of newly learned words?

9. Frequently engage in discussions about vocabulary?

10. Understand analogies and engage in conversations about word relationships?

Have fun learning vocabulary. Words really are magic. Extensive vocabularies improve our ability to communicate orally, assist in reading comprehension, and make for more precise and interesting writing. Encourage your students to read extensively and to be curious about words. Teach words—it works!

CHAPTER 7

SPELLING IN GRADES FOUR, FIVE, AND SIX

The one best way to teach spelling is to know each student in your classroom as a speller. Ask yourself:

1. Is learning to spell new words correctly difficult or easy for this student?
2. What is the student's present level of spelling ability—above grade level, on grade level, or below grade level?
3. What are the student's spelling habits in writing?

Is spelling difficult or easy? A fourth-, fifth-, and sixth-grade teacher must know whether correct spelling comes fairly naturally and easily for the student or whether he or she struggles to spell perfectly even after study and effort. Some children have a natural ability to spell, but about one in five are naturally poor spellers. The difference in ability goes beyond whether the learner is an auditory learner or a visual learner. The naturally good speller has a mental capacity to "see" the word in his or her mind's eye. This ability is sometimes called "a visual coding mechanism." In some ways, expert spellers may be born, not made. I often marvel at a 13-year-old who can spell *cappeletti* at a national spelling bee and wonder how I ended up at the other end of the spectrum. Just as some children are musically predisposed with perfect pitch while others can't carry a tune, some children seem to have a natural ability to spell while others, like myself, will always struggle with spelling.

What level of instruction is best? You must know each student's spelling instructional level, differentiating instruction for varying levels of word knowledge. A child who spells on a fifth-grade level needs to learn different words and patterns than a child who spells on a second-grade level. Your job is to match each student in your classroom with words and patterns that are appropriate for him or her. Effective study of fifth-grade words and patterns assumes an underlying knowledge base of simpler words and patterns as well as supporting knowledge about the general way English spelling works. For example, it makes sense to learn more frequently used words such as *house, very, many, little, some, give, after,* and *put* (second-grade level words) before studying words such as *rectangular, bargain, vanish, modern, burglar, habit,* and *prison* (fifth-grade level words). It makes sense for students to understand letter patterns within single-syllable words such as *hop, heat,* and *hope* before they grasp the "double-consonant" and "drop e" principles when adding suffixes (*hop + ing = hopping;* hope + *ing = hoping*). These concepts should probably be learned before students learn that words derived from a common root word maintain the spelling of the root (*oppose, opposition*).

Are good spelling habits apparent? You must know each student's spelling habits when he or she writes. Is the student developing an appropriate habit of care for spelling? Spelling consciousness and good spelling habits must be taught. Otherwise, the end result may be good spellers with sloppy spelling habits.

Spelling is complex. I have studied spelling education for over 30 years, conducted research, worked with teachers, and written instructional materials and best-selling books on the teaching of spelling. Many teachers begin to improve spelling instruction once they shed five commonly held false assumptions.

FIVE FALSE ASSUMPTIONS ABOUT SPELLING INSTRUCTION

1. All children can become expert spellers if they try hard enough. The ones who do not are probably lazy.
2. Children who attain 100% on a spelling test should be able to spell the same words correctly two weeks later in their writing.
3. Expert spelling is "caught" from reading and writing and is best taught only in meaningful context.
4. Spelling instruction is simple. Just focus on a few high-frequency words.
5. Spelling doesn't matter.

1. All children can become expert spellers if they try hard enough. The ones who do not are probably lazy.

Spelling is not based solely on intelligence, experience, education, and effort. While literate students who work at it can become better spellers, to expect all students to be expert spellers is as unlikely as expecting every teacher who reads this book to become an accomplished opera singer. A number of factors are at work in determining spelling ability, including an innate ability to "see" words in the mind's eye. New brain research may be unraveling some of the mysteries and complexities of spelling, including the fact that spelling may even have a neurological basis. Italian, French, and British researchers, for example, conducted brain scans on struggling versus normal spellers and found little activity in brain areas linking language to visual cues among the struggling spellers. (Paulesu, et. al., 2001)

Accept the fact that some students will struggle with spelling. Your goal should be to help each student become a better speller and to develop good spelling habits.

2. Children who attain 100% on a spelling test should be able to spell the same words correctly two weeks later in their writing.

This might be true for about four out of five students. About 20% of your students will misspell some of the words they memorized for the spelling test. That does not mean the effort to teach and learn spelling was ineffective. Students who struggle with learning spelling may improve their ability even though they may not retain all the words studied. As we have seen, a number of factors work together to determine spelling ability. You should expect to encounter some students who attained 100% on the test but continue to misspell some of the same words in their writing a few weeks later. These misspelled words should be recycled. Additionally, a periodic review of learned words should be an expected routine of spelling instruction. Some students are unable to transfer spelling skills into writing simply because it's very difficult for them to retain the visual form of the word in their brains. It remains unclear whether seeing words in the mind's eye is a skill that can be taught.

3. Expert spelling is "caught" from reading and writing and is best taught only in meaningful context.

> "'Don't worry, his spelling will improve when he reads more!' This is one of the many myths that surround the spelling skill. He will not, in fact, just 'catch' spelling by reading."
>
> (Peters, 1985, p. 25)

There have been a number of periods in fairly recent history when teachers stopped teaching spelling in favor of the notion that expert spelling is an incidental result when students read and write a lot. One such period was during the 1960s in Great Britain when "creative writing" became fashionable. Out of that era came a remarkable little book by a spelling researcher that, for me, put an end to the speculation that spelling is "caught." Originally published in 1967, the classic textbook

Spelling: Caught or Taught? by Margaret L. Peters, a former lecturer in literacy at the Cambridge Institute of Education in London, presents research on the issue and shows that it has been known for some time "that a great many children do not manage to 'catch' spelling as they learn to read."

A popular offshoot of the "spelling is caught" theory is the notion that the best way to teach spelling is to focus on writing and teach spelling in use. Essentially, this means teach spelling "off the top of your head" at the "teachable moment" as students write.

Certainly teachers must help students connect spelling to writing. It makes no sense if the two aren't connected because the very purpose of spelling education in grades four, five, and six is for students to develop word-specific knowledge needed to spell words correctly in writing. I always recommend teaching words and patterns students use in their writing in grades four, five, and six. However, connecting spelling to writing is a different issue and separate from focusing on writing and teaching spelling in use.

A problem with teaching spelling only in meaningful context is that at about third-grade level word-specific knowledge becomes very specialized. This method requires the teacher to come up with good lessons or examples of spelling patterns off the top of his or her head. You can probably quickly think of many words that rhyme with *rat*, but how quickly can you think of words that end in *-ible*? Can you think of six pronunciations of the spelling pattern *-ough*? (*through, rough, cough, plough, thorough,* and *hiccough*.) Teaching spelling well requires planning and resources. It can't simply be "anticipated" and delivered "off the top of your head" at "teachable moments" (Laminack and Wood, 1996, p. 65). It would be nice, for example, to teach homophones at a teachable moment when 25 writers need to use *principal* versus *principle* by teaching the mini-lesson "the princi*pal* is my *pal*." The problem is that there are over 500 high-frequency homophones that fourth-, fifth-, and sixth-grade writers use, and teaching homophones is only a fraction of the spelling curriculum in grades four, five, and six.

If you did include an appropriate spelling curriculum in your teaching as you focus on writing, you would never get around to teaching writing. Spellings, such as the 500 homophones that your students use, are not learned just one at a time, nor are they learned just from reading. English spelling is complex. To develop adequate word-specific knowledge and function as good writers most students require a systematic study of words and patterns and a deep understanding of the intricacies of the English spelling system.

4. Spelling instruction is simple. Just focus on a few high-frequency words.

To suggest that focusing on high-frequency words will result in correct spelling doesn't work. Programs that teach the high-use writing words in the order of their frequency typically focus on some arbitrary number of high-frequency words such as "the high-use 500" or "1,200 high-use writing words." The central problem with this methodology is that only a very limited number of high-frequency words are studied. What about the *other* words and spelling patterns? I have met many sixth graders who have memorized the 1,200 most frequently used words yet remain inadequate spellers.

Another problem is that instruction tends to get stuck on "easy" words long after these words should have been mastered. Learning high-frequency words and how to spell them is important. However, it's the high-frequency word notion taken to the extreme.

Finally, there is much research to discredit programs that focus on one aspect of spelling and shortchange the importance of other aspects, such as spelling patterns or presentation of a few good spelling rules. Certainly the underlying knowledge used by all expert spellers includes knowledge of patterns, knowledge of spellings that are associated with sounds, and knowledge of some rules. Students need to acquire this knowledge. For example, a solid fifth-grade lesson might present this word list: *motion, magician, vacation, electrician, condition, musician, composition, direction, section,* and *physician.* A word sort might lead the students to discover that words ending in *-tion* name things and words ending in *-cian* name people. Students might learn the rule that the /shun/ sound at the end of a word is never spelled *shun.* Word sorting helps students learn something about probability—if they are sorting words with the /a-shun/ sound at the end of a word, they should notice that the vast majority (more than 1,200 words) are spelled *-ation.* Only four words with the /a-shun/ sound at the end have other spellings. This word-specific knowledge is more helpful for the fifth grader than simply memorizing the spellings of some arbitrary number of most frequently used words.

A number of other misguided beliefs may lead to simplistic and inadequate practices. Avoid any one technique that is supposed to be a cure-all. While word sorting is an effective instructional strategy, it was not designed to supplant a spelling curriculum. For example, in the preface of *Words Their Way,* an excellent resource for word sorting, the authors explain " . . . *Words Their Way* complements the use of any existing phonics, spelling, and vocabulary curricula." (Bear, Invernizzi, Templeton, and Johnston, 2000, p. V)

Word sorting is a powerful activity for learning word-specific knowledge but it has limitations. It takes a lot of time to do whole-class and small-group word sorts, which reduces the time for reading, writing, or individualized spelling instruction. Additionally, I doubt word sorting has been sufficiently tested to allow it to replace more individualized techniques.

My personal experience with word sorting is quite remarkable. In my seminars I often have teachers sort the following words into two categories that end up like this:

worshiping	forgetting
traveling	permitted
canceling	submitted
credited	preferring
budgeted	occurred

I ask the teachers to come up with a generalization that describes the dynamics of this word sort. About one in 10 teachers will come up with the correct generalization: If the accent is on the second syllable, double the consonant when adding the suffix; if the accent is on the first syllable, do not double the consonant. But here's what I find remarkable. After demonstrating this word sort on scores of occasions, I will sometimes come across the spelling of one of these words in my writing and I don't know how to spell it! After all these years, the word sort has neither taught me the rule or the automatic spelling of these words.

Sometimes teachers who have invested a great deal of time and effort into developing a set of procedures for teaching spelling have met their goals with some success. "Why should I make changes?" they ask. In this circumstance, I invite teachers to go beyond what's comfortable and be a lifelong learner. I ask teachers not to be smug when it comes to how best to teach spelling. Unless you know each student in your classroom individually as a speller, and unless you are meeting his or her needs, your methodology is not working as well as you think.

Still another oversimplification is the notion that all spelling textbook programs are bad. Spelling basals bring two absolutely essential resources to a district: first, a spelling curriculum and second, resources to make teaching spelling easier. These resources help teachers choose the right words and patterns for study and provide easy access to instructional activities or mini-lessons. Basals eliminate the "do your own thing" phenomenon, which too often leaves fourth-grade teachers without a record of words and patterns their students studied last year in third grade. When used appropriately, good spelling basals make it easier to differentiate instruction and to know each speller individually.

We all know spelling basals have been misused: some students who were forced to do workbook pages in spelling programs didn't learn to spell well; basals have taken up time that would best be spent reading and writing; and the spending costs for spelling books eat into the school budget. Nevertheless, spelling books may be needed in most schools. When I visit schools that don't have them, I find spelling education is being neglected or spelling is poorly taught.

5. Spelling doesn't matter.

When I ask students whether or not their teachers think spelling is important, they sometimes report, "We don't do much spelling in class." or "My teacher says just use the spell check." There are other telltale signs that the school district doesn't value spelling: no spelling curriculum; no spelling resources for teachers; no time for spelling in the schedule; and no reporting of a child's spelling progress to his or her parents.

Some say computers make learning spelling obsolete. I believe just the opposite. Computer tools such as a spell check are a great boon to spelling education. But in some ways computers make reliance on expert spelling more important. Try to find Hutchenreuther china on e-Bay if you don't know how to spell it or pop the name Robsjohn-Gibbings in your search engine by typing Robesjon or Gibbons—you won't get very far. Have you ever become frustrated with your computer spell check? A college student who was writing his thesis complained to me, "Sometimes the spell check on my computer starts acting stupid!" The notion that good spelling is obsolete may itself be stupid. There is still a stigma attached to poor spelling, and like it or not, ignoring correct spelling can have serious real-life consequences.

Many of the best examples I find to support this fact are anecdotal. For example, employees of Bill Gates' Microsoft tell me they get hundreds of Ph.D. applications over the Internet. They use an unofficial policy to screen the applications: Any application with a spelling error is eliminated. Then there is the parent who told me that her son wanted to go to the Coast Guard Academy. When they visited the college, an admissions officer explained his unofficial policy for screening applications: "I first look at the application for spelling errors. Anyone who has misspelled *Coast Guard Academy* gets rejected," which is about one-third of the applicants! Some very capable students probably get rejected because no one taught them that in the real world spelling is important.

THE SPELLING WORKSHOP

The spelling workshop is a 15-minute period each day when you turn your fourth-, fifth-, or sixth-grade classroom into a community of learners who are becoming better spellers. Your students should emerge from the spelling workshop each Friday with new word-specific knowledge to use when they write. This is knowledge that they did not have on the previous Monday.

A typical Monday through Friday schedule includes the following routines:

Monday—Students take a pretest on the weekly words in the curriculum from their spelling book. They self-correct the pretest and collect any misspelled words. (See page 132.)

Tuesday—Students construct their own list of 10 words, gleaning some words from the Monday pretest and words misspelled in their writing. (See page 133.)

Wednesday and Thursday—Students follow prescribed routines, either individually or with buddies, to master the 10 words on their lists. The teacher may conduct whole-group or small-group mini-lessons if performance on the Monday pretest indicated a need for further instruction. (See page 134.)

Friday—Students follow routines with a spelling partner for taking a final test on the words they have studied. The teacher corrects the final test. (See page 137.)

I believe "best spelling practice" means individualizing instruction and knowing the students in your classroom individually as spellers. Many school districts are returning to basal spelling programs to bring a curriculum and teaching resources back into the classroom. This section will show how to use a basal to individualize your classroom program and provide differentiated instruction. The objectives of the individualized, writing-based spelling program are:

- Adapt spelling instruction according to the needs of each individual.
- Focus on words that the student cannot spell.
- Connect spelling with writing.
- Provide ongoing spelling assessment and learning.
- Raise the student's consciousness of spelling strategies and good spelling habits in writing.

Devote about 15 minutes on spelling within a two to two and one-half hour literacy block. Your work with spelling will be greatly enhanced and more efficient if you teach writing to the same students to whom you are teaching spelling. Begin your preparation for spelling instruction by looking at the way each student handles spelling in writing.

ASSESSMENT ACTIVITY: STUDENT WRITING

Since your goal is to know each student as a speller as soon as possible, begin the year by looking at a few pages of rough-draft writing from each student to acquaint yourself with that student as a speller. Look only at spelling—not punctuation, sentence structure, word choice, or meaning—to determine classroom groupings for spelling instruction. Contrast the misspelled words with the words in the spelling book to predict how well the writer will match with the spelling curriculum. Ask yourself: "Do I find evidence of above-grade level, on-grade level, or below-grade level spelling performance?" The answer will help you begin to think about your class in terms of instructional subgroups. Sort the writing samples into three stacks based on the level of the words misspelled: grade-level spellers, below-grade-level spellers, and above-grade-level spellers. Initial groupings are flexible and will change as you get to know students better and can focus more accurately on their performance and motivation. Sometimes there are only two groups. In other cases, four groups emerge: above-, on, below-grade level, and possibly one small group of two or three individuals who are severely disabled spellers. This initial classroom survey of spelling in writing will begin to help you form a picture of how spelling study will be organized for the year.

The fifth-grade samples in Figures 7.1 and 7.2 demonstrate how information about the individuals can be gleaned from this quick, informal assessment based on writing. The "think aloud" after each sample models determining the student's initial group placement.

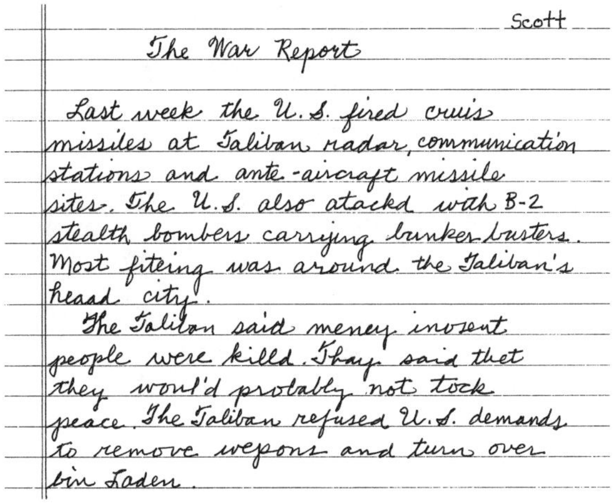
Scott

The War Report

Last week the U.S. fired cruis missiles at Taliban radar, communication stations and ante-aircraft missile sites. The U.S. also atackd with B-2 stealth bombers carrying bunker busters. Most fiteing was around the Taliban's heaad city.

The Talibon said meney inosent people were killd. Thay said thet they woul'd probably not tock peace. The Taliban refused U.S. demands to remove wepons and turn over bin Laden.

Figure 7.1

Gentry think aloud: Scott is a struggling speller. I already see clear evidence of a hodgepodge of invented spelling strategies and below-grade level functioning. I anticipate that Scott will need instruction in spelling that is well below-grade level this year. I plan to work with Scott individually or in a small group of other struggling spellers.

Scott may be one of about 2% of people who have a fairly severe spelling disability. If my work with him confirms this, I will need to provide special supervision to support Scott's spelling growth. For example, I may become Scott's editor for spelling this year with the objective of making sure he forms the habit of always getting help with spelling when he intends the piece to be read by others. I will try to build up Scott's confidence as a writer and help him recognize that while he may not be a naturally good speller, he can continue to improve both as a speller and a writer.

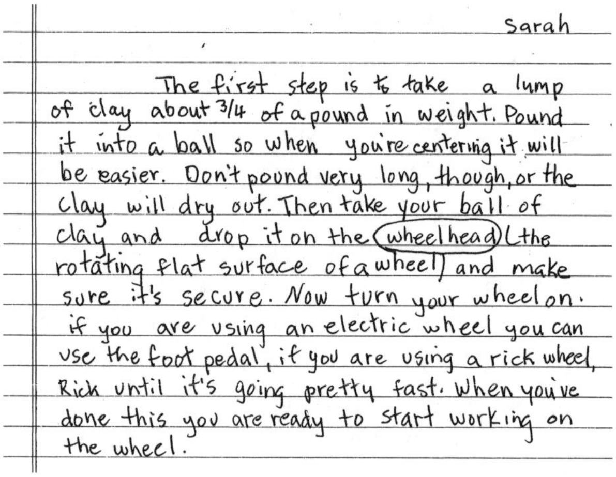

Sarah

The first step is to take a lump of clay about 3/4 of a pound in weight. Pound it into a ball so when you're centering it will be easier. Don't pound very long, though, or the clay will dry out. Then take your ball of clay and drop it on the (wheelhead) (the rotating flat surface of a wheel) and make sure it's secure. Now turn your wheel on. If you are using an electric wheel you can use the foot pedal, if you are using a rick wheel, Rick until it's going pretty fast. When you've done this you are ready to start working on the wheel.

Figure 7.2

Gentry think aloud: Sarah seems to be a good speller. She will fit nicely into a grade-level spelling group. She's conscious of spelling in her writing and demonstrates good spelling habits, such as circling words she's not sure of as she writes. She uses this strategy without disrupting her train of thought. She's a natural speller, on-grade level, with good spelling habits.

Sometimes I find writing samples that indicate students are excellent or superior spellers. They may spell very obscure words correctly and use the computer spell check with no prompting. These spellers are natural spellers, above-grade level, with good spelling habits. Their instruction is largely individualized and may be well above-grade level.

ASSESSMENT ACTIVITY: INFORMAL SPELLING INVENTORY

During the first two weeks of school, administer an informal spelling assessment, such as The Gentry Spelling Grade Level Placement Test (See the Appendix, page 191). Each student is tested on several consecutive grade level lists. If the student spells about half of the words on the list correctly, that is the student's approximate instructional grade level for spelling. Usually it requires three or four lists to determine a student's level. For example, if a student receives 100% on the fourth-grade list, 75% on the fifth-grade list, 55% on the sixth-grade list, and 40% on the seventh-grade list, the student's approximate instructional spelling level is sixth grade. Use the following procedure.

Day 1: Administer the grade-level list. Score the papers. Students who scored 50% or higher will get the next higher-grade level list on Day 2. Students who scored 45% or lower will get the next lower-grade level list on Day 2. (There are 20 words on each list so all scores will be in 5% increments.)

Day 2: Administer the 50% and above student group the next higher-grade level list. Any students who get 50% or above at this grade level will go to the next higher-grade level the next day (i.e., two levels above grade level). Stop testing each student when he or she reaches the highest-grade level at which he or she scores close to 50%.

Administer the next lower-grade level list to students who were in the 45% or lower range on the grade-level list. Continue to work backwards with this group, administering the next lower-grade level list until these students reach the level at which they score close to 50% correct on a list.

The Gentry Spelling Grade Level Placement Test is just one indicator of each student's grade level of spelling proficiency. Use the results in conjunction with your observations of what the student does with spelling in writing to help you do a better job of matching students with the best words for instruction.

Use information from the informal spelling assessment to supplement the initial classroom groupings based on writing samples. You may end up with three instructional groups and one or two students who are either severely disabled spellers or exceptional spellers. Plan to guide these students individually or with a spelling buddy who has comparable ability.

GETTING STARTED WITH SPELLING WORKSHOP

After the assessment activities have informed you about each student as a speller, you are ready to form three general instructional level groups (above-grade level, on-grade level, and below-grade level). Assess all three groups each Monday on 10 appropriate pretest words. While the pretest words for each group will be different, the spelling strategy or pattern to be studied each week will be the same for everyone in the classroom. Here's an example:

> One week in a fourth-grade spelling workshop students might study different spellings of the r-controlled vowel in words, such as *clerk*, *shirt*, and *hurt*. The below-grade level group pretest words might be *bird*, *birthday*, *fur*, and *turn*; The on-grade level group pretest words might be *clerk*, *circus*, *turtle*, and *burst*; The

above-grade level group pretest words might be *burglar, current, further,* and *twirl.* (Gentry, Harris, Graham, and Zutell, 1998, *Spell It—Write!* Grade 4, p. T118)

Students may move to a higher or lower group depending on their pretest results three weeks in a row. For example, students in a below-grade level group who receive 100% on the pretest three Mondays in a row move up to the grade-level list. Students who miss more that half the words on pretests three weeks in a row move to a lower list.

INDIVIDUAL SPELLING JOURNALS—
THE WINK LIST (WORDS I NEED TO KNOW)

During the first week of school, each student brings in a slim notebook to write words he or she needs to know how to spell. The main purpose of the spelling journal is to build spelling consciousness by having the student get in the habit of looking for words he or she can't spell in writing. There are at least five ways to find words for the journal: "green-penning" words in student writing; pretesting and assigning content words; words chosen by the student from his or her writing; words gleaned from "word hunts" conducted by the student; and recycling words that are misspelled on weekly spelling tests.

TEACHING ACTIVITY: GREEN-PENNING WORDS

Green-penning is used by the teacher to maintain ongoing assessment of each student as a speller and, at the same time, helps each student find unknown spelling words. In addition to pretesting on a short list of appropriate words each week, green-penning is the primary way a teacher may match students with words tailored for them. I use green ink because green signals *go.*

> Keep a green ink pen with you at all times. If you spot a developmentally appropriate, high-frequency word misspelled in a student's writing, circle the word and write it correctly in green at the bottom of the page. Look for these words in anything the child writes. When the child sees a word you have written in green, it means "put this word in your spelling journal." Green-pen two pages of each child's writing at least once every three weeks. Green-penning is for spelling only. Editing is a separate process. (Gentry, September 1997, "Spelling Strategies," *Instructor,* New York: Scholastic. p. 77 and *The Literacy Map (K-3),* 2000)

TEACHING ACTIVITY: CONTENT-WORDS PRETEST

Often, students are required to learn to spell certain content words. These may be history words, geography words, math words, or others prescribed by the local curriculum. It takes about 15 minutes of content-area time to pretest these words. You may introduce the activity in the following way: "In the next three weeks we will be studying weather. We'll use words such as *precipitation* and *meteorologist*. Today we will have a pretest on some of the content words you will be using. If you misspell any of these words, add them to your WINK list (Words I Need to Know). Put a star beside these words to remind you to give them priority." Add these words to your weekly spelling list over the next three weeks.

TEACHING ACTIVITY: STUDENT-SELECTED WORDS

Once a week at a designated time in writer's workshop, have students find words in their own writing that may be misspelled. Ask students to add these words to their spelling journals. The routine takes about 5 to 10 minutes a week. Display the following steps on a chart as a reminder for students:

1. Circle three words on your draft that may be misspelled.
2. Try spelling the words again by visualizing the word, spelling the word the way it sounds, or spelling the word by analogy to another word you know.
3. Find the correct spelling by asking someone, looking up the word, or using a computer spell check.
4. Add the words to the WINK list (Words I Need to Know).

(Gentry, 1997 and 2000)

TEACHING ACTIVITY: WORD HUNT

Hunting for spelling words may be a whole class or individual homework assignment for students who need to add more words to their WINK lists. Begin by explaining to students that you want them to choose 10 new words for their spelling journal. Tell them that they should choose words they use in their writing but are not sure how to spell correctly or automatically. Remind students that the best words are words they use often. "*Akhenaton* is not the kind of word you are hunting for. You can't use that word in your everyday writing. Look for familiar words."

Model word hunting to show students how to find words that match the level of the words you have been green-penning for them. "If I green-penned words like *into*, *bluebird*, and *which*, would *ineligible*, *irascible*, and *hiccough* be a good match for you? If I green-pen words like *thorough* and *irrepressible* for you, what do you think I will say if you choose words like *cat*, *dog*, and *fish*?"

Do a quick check to see that the words students choose are an appropriate match to their spelling grade-level list. Have them add the 10 new words to their WINK lists. Take note of super spellers who need to create very advanced lists. For example, if a fourth grader can spell on eighth-grade level and he has a rottweiler at home that he likes to write about, the word *rottweiler* may be a good word for his list.

TEACHING ACTIVITY: CHARTING TECHNICAL WORDS

While there is an expectation for correct spelling of technical or content-specific words in students' writing, it should not be required of students to memorize the spellings of such words. For example, the words *Nefertiti*, *Tutankhamen*, *hieroglyphs*, and *sarcophagus* related to a study of Egypt may be displayed on a wall chart for easy reference. Remind students to use the wall chart before handing in their papers.

I do challenge students to memorize the spellings of obscure content words just for fun and interest. I never stifle a student's natural curiosity or inclination to challenge him- or herself with difficult spelling words as long as those words aren't taking away from time spent studying more frequently used words.

MANAGING THE SPELLING WORKSHOP
(15 minutes a day—a five-day cycle)

The spelling workshop—an individualized, writing-based spelling program—differs from the traditional spelling program that requires all students to study the same words and may not connect well to misspelled words in the students' writing. But don't toss out your traditional basal just yet. You may use the basal to provide the resources you need for spelling workshop. You will use it flexibly rather than follow a traditional procedure or assign workbook pages. The basal is a teaching resource that should make your job easier.

Keep in mind that most spelling basals are organized around a corpus of words that were based on research studies of writers at your grade level. These studies help to identify those words and spelling patterns writers at a particular grade level actually use. For example, over 20 studies were consulted in compiling the word list for the spelling basal, *Spelling Connections* (Gentry, 2000c, p. Z15).

In the spelling workshop everyone in the class studies a "big idea" that is part of the grade-level curriculum. This may be a particular high-use and grade-level appropriate spelling pattern or a spelling strategy. Your spelling textbook makes planning for this aspect of the workshop effortless. All the resources are provided: appropriate words for study, a curriculum, ideas for engaging students with the words, and mini-lessons and teaching tips. In the spelling workshop, the individual needs of each student are addressed as students glean words to be studied from their spelling journals.

Each week students follow a routine for building a spelling list of unknown spelling words that is just right for each one of them. Words found misspelled in the student's writing are added to his or her WINK list. Another part of the routine is finding words to be studied by pretesting from a curriculum of spelling words from the spelling book. Students then develop a "split word list"—up to half of the list for a week is comprised of pretest words and the remainder is from the student's personal spelling journal. Students who do not miss pretest words choose all the words from their spelling journal. Unlike the traditional 20-word spelling list method, this routine will insure that words studied are always unknown, having been misspelled either on a pretest or in the student's writing.

THE PERFECT WORD LIST

The key to having each student successfully manage his or her own word list is to keep the list short enough to handle in a 15-minute daily workshop but long enough to impact the child's development of word-specific knowledge. When compared to a traditional 20-word spelling list, the shorter spelling list is an example of "less is more." Advantages include ease of management and efficiency. All 10 words being studied in the spelling workshop are unknown words. Typically children who are well-matched to a traditional list already can correctly spell half of the words on the list. In fact, when placing children in traditional spelling programs, the appropriate grade level for instruction is the level at which the child already spells about half of the words correctly. (Henderson, *Learning to Read and Spell: The Child's Knowledge of Words*, 1981) Hypothetically, a fifth grader who spells on a fifth-grade level will get 20 words for the week. He already knows the correct spelling of half of them. He spends about half the spelling time—pretesting, studying, using the words in exercises, taking the final test—with words he already knows how to spell. In contrast, all 10 words in the writing-based, individualized spelling program designed for spelling workshop are unknown words. Students do not waste time working with words they can already spell and manage the list in half the time that would be needed for a 20-word list.

A WORD ABOUT ROUTINES

The secret to successful management of individualized spelling lists in spelling workshop is the secret for all good classroom management: establish clear schedules, routines, and expectations so students know exactly what to do and when to do it.

Expectations should be well-established and practiced before your students carry out the routines on their own. If the daily routines occur at precisely the same time for each day of spelling workshop, management flows even more smoothly. The expectation, the routine, and the time when it occurs are all explicitly modeled by the teacher and completely understood by each student. The following schedule models a five-day spelling workshop.

DAY 1: PRETEST AND SELF-CORRECTION (Monday, 10:45-11:00)

Day 1 is the day for a preliminary assessment of each student's knowledge of the pattern or strategy being studied in the week's spelling workshop. I often refer to the pretest as *a spelling check* to see whether writers understand a set of words or patterns that are used often. The Monday spelling check includes a research-based practice, having each child correct his or her own pretest.

Gentry: O.K. students, it's 10:45. Please put away your writing workshop materials. It's time for spelling workshop. Today is Monday, so we'll have our spelling check. I'll be checking your spelling knowledge to see if you can spell a list of compound words that fifth-grade students like you use often and need to know how to spell.

Take a sheet of paper and number it from 1 to 10. I will pretest each spelling group on 10 compound words. When we complete the pretest, we will use the circle-dot strategy (see page 133) to have you check your own work.

If you misspell any words, congratulations! You have found some of the words you will be learning to spell perfectly this week. As you know, our goal today is to find some new words you can learn to spell perfectly and automatically.

Once the routine is established, it's easy to administer spelling checks to three groups who are functioning at different levels with compound words. Spelling textbooks may provide a below-grade level list of compound words, a list of 10 grade-level compound words, and an above-grade level list of compound words. I usually designate the lists by colors and while the red list group is writing their word, I call out the blue list word, use it in a sentence, then go on to the green list. After calling out the green list word, the original red list group is ready for their next word. Some teachers do all the words for one group's list before proceeding to the next group. Both procedures can be completed in about 10 minutes, leaving time for students to self-correct using the circle-dot strategy.

A good research-based spelling program should provide all the resources you need. If your spelling text doesn't have a below- and above-grade level-list for each unit find the comparable list in the spelling books for the next lower and next higher-grade levels. At the end of the pretests, have students use the circle-dot strategy to check their own pretests. Having students check their own pretest helps them learn the perfect spelling.

TEACHING ACTIVITY: CIRCLE-DOT STRATEGY

As you or a student group leader spells aloud each pretest word correctly, have students put a dot under each correct letter and a circle to mark each spelling error. A circle may be drawn to show where a letter was left out or drawn around each incorrect letter. The circles show the speller visually where each error is located. (See *The Literacy Map: Guiding Children to Where They Need to Be (K-3)*, 2000, pp. 121-122.)

DAY 2: MAKE THE WORD LISTS (Tuesday, 10:45-11:00)

On Day 2 each student makes his or her own individual word list. Each student starts the list with misspelled pretest words and completes it with words from his or her spelling journal (WINK list). This split-list routine is accompanied by instructions for making two copies of the week's spelling list—one to leave at school and one to take home. The child makes his or her 10-word spelling list for the week on a sheet of paper with two columns labeled *School* and *Home*, copying the list twice. Students fold the paper in half, cut it along the fold, and leave one list at school with the teacher, eliminating the possibility of losing individual word lists.

The first routine for Day 2 is for each student to choose up to five words for their list from words missed on the Monday spelling check. If no words were missed they proceed to the second routine described below. If more than five words were missed on the Monday pretest, students choose five of the missed words. Depending upon the number of words missed on Monday, students may have from zero to five of the pretest words to begin their list for a particular week's study.

The second routine for Day 2 is to complete the list by adding words from the WINK list to compile 10 words. These words need not match the pattern being focused on in the weekly workshop; rather, the words are any words the student chooses to learn.

When selecting a word from the spelling journal to add to the list, the student crosses through the word in the journal to indicate it will be studied and mastered. If the word is misspelled on the Friday test it goes back on the WINK list. If the word is memorized for the test but later found misspelled in writing, it is green-penned, recycled, and again appears in the spelling journal. Crossing a line through a word to be learned and reentering it if it is later misspelled is a record-keeping device to help the student and teacher determine whether words being studied are being transferred into the student's daily writing. This simple routine raises the student's level of consciousness for correct spelling in writing of words that have been learned for the spelling test.

DAYS 3 AND 4: MINI-LESSONS AND INDIVIDUAL OR BUDDY SESSIONS (Wednesday and Thursday, 10:45-11:00)

Days 3 and 4 are instructional and word study days. Activities may include whole-class or small-group word sorting activities led by the teacher for those students whose pretest results indicated a need for work on the current pattern or strategy being studied. Students who have demonstrated competence with the pattern or strategy choose from a variety of independent activities to study and practice the words on their individual lists. Below you will find whole group and independent routines often used on Days 3 and 4.

TEACHING ACTIVITY: WORD SORTS

Word sorting is a research-based activity that works particularly well with both whole class and small groups. (Zutell, "Word Sorting: A Developmental Spelling Approach to Word Study for Delayed Readers." *Reading and Writing Quarterly*, 14 #2, April-June, 1998, pp. 219-238) It allows students to organize words into categories based on shared features. The words are printed on individual word cards and arranged into columns. Spelling word sorts may be based on various word study features, allowing students to contrast words according to the sound, spelling patterns, or meaning units. The activity goes beyond rote memorization and allows students to form concepts about the general system of how English spelling works. Words are not only learned as single entities but also in relation to one another. For example, students learn general system concepts such as the vowel-consonant-e pattern in which silent *e* signals that the vowel is likely to be long (*make*, *ate*, and *cake*). Word sorts help students remember spellings as they form associations among similarly spelled words. The activity also helps them learn the probability that certain spelling patterns are frequent while other patterns are rare (long *a* spelled *eigh*). The instructional power of word sorting resides in the fact that sorts are multi-modal (visual, auditory, kinesthetic, tactile), manipulative, collaborative, and accessible for modeling and demonstration.

Word sorts in grades four, five, and six should match the level of word-specific knowledge of the learner. Patterns used frequently at early stages should be studied before patterns typical of later development. Keep in mind that the number of categories in a word sort may vary and that most spelling word sorts include a category for "exceptions." Below are three word sorts that might be taught in mini-lessons in fourth, fifth, and sixth grade spelling workshops.

A FOURTH-GRADE WORD SORT

This word sort was designed for a fourth-grade spelling workshop lesson based on the *dge* and *ge* pattern: When the /j/ sound comes right after a short vowel sound, it is usually spelled *dge*, as in *bridge*. When the /j/ sound comes right after a long vowel sound, it is usually spelled *ge*, as in *stage*.

Sort the pattern words into three groups. Write the pattern word under the guide word that has the same sound and spelling pattern. If a word doesn't fit with a guide word put it in the question mark group.

bridge (short vowel + *dge*)	stage (long vowel + *ge*)	? (other vowel + *ge*)
badge	rage	charge
judge	strange	
edge	engage	

(Adapted from *Spell It—Write!*, Grade 4)

A FIFTH-GRADE WORD SORT

This word sort was designed for a fifth-grade spelling workshop based on the concept that some prefixes indicate amount or position. You can make a new word by adding prefixes, such as *bi-*, *tri-*, *mid-* and *semi-* to a base word.

bi-	*tri-*	*mid-*	*semi-*
bicycle	triangle	midnight	semicircle
biweekly	tricycle	midstream	semisweet
bifocals		midafternoon	

(Adapted from *Spell It—Write!*, Grade 5)

A SIXTH-GRADE WORD SORT

This word sort was designed for a sixth-grade spelling workshop based on the concept that many words begin with the prefixes *extra-*, *inter-*, and *intra-*. The prefix *extra-* means "outside" or "beyond." The prefix *inter-* means "between," and *intra-* means "within."

inter-	*extra-*	*intra-*
interfere	extravagant	intrastate
interview	extracurricular	intramural
intermediate	extraterrestrial	

(Adapted from *Spell It—Write!*, Grade 6)

TEACHING ACTIVITY: INDEPENDENT/PARTNER STRATEGIES

Students who have demonstrated competence with the pattern or strategy choose from a variety of independent or partner activities to study and practice the words on their individual list. The following two activities from *Spell It—Write! Spelling Process Handbook* (Gentry, et. al., Zaner-Bloser, 1998) illustrate possibilities for individual and partner work. Other activities, such as game mats, help students practice their individual spelling lists while playing board games and using markers to earn points.

With a Partner

 Spelling Tic-Tac-Toe

1. Find a partner. Draw a tic-tac-toe grid on a piece of paper.
2. Trade spelling lists. Make sure you can read all the words on each other's lists.
3. Decide who will go first. (It's best to take turns going first.) Decide who will use X and who will use O.
4. Say the first word on your partner's list out loud. Your partner should spell the word out loud while you use his list to check the spelling. If your partner is correct, he should write either X or O (whichever he is using) on the tic-tac-toe grid. If your partner is not right, spell the word correctly—out loud and one letter at a time—for your partner.
5. Trade jobs. Your partner will say a word from your spelling list and you will try to spell it. If you are right, make an X or O (whichever you are using) on the board. If you are not correct, your partner will spell your word out loud.
6. Keep taking turns until you or your partner makes~three X's or three O's in a line on the board. If you fill up the board before either of you makes a line, start again.

On Your Own

Spelling Study Strategy

Look, Say, Cover, See, Write, Check, Rewrite

1. Look at the word you want to learn.
2. Say the word.
3. Cover the word. See the word in your mind. (You may want to close your eyes.)
4. Write the word.
5. Check your spelling.
6. Rewrite the word correctly.

Flip Folder

1. Get a **Flip Folder** and **Flip Folder** Practice Sheet.
2. Print your spelling list in the first column. Check to see that you spelled each word correctly.
3. Slide your Practice Sheet into the **Flip Folder**.
4. Open Flap 1.
   - Look at the first word.
   - Say the word.
5. Close Flap 1.
   - See the word in your mind. (You may want to close your eyes.)
6. Open Flap 2.
   - Write the word on the first line.
7. Open Flap 1 and Flap 2 at the same time.
   - Check your spelling.
8. Open Flap 3.
   - Write the word again.
9. Open Flaps 1 and 3 at the same time.
   - Check your spelling.

DAY 5: PARTNER QUIZZES (Friday, 10:45–11:00)

Students quiz each other on their individual word lists on Day 5 of the cycle. The shorter word list makes it possible for students to manage this aspect of the spelling workshop easily within the 15-minute block and allows time for the teacher to check each test on the spot.

Begin by establishing a weekly routine for bringing spelling partners together for assessment. Create cards with individual student names on them. Shuffle the cards and draw pairs randomly to determine who will work together. Remind students to bring their lists for the week to the class meeting area. The list must be neat and readable. If it contains homophones, such as *our* and *hour*, the student draws a picture clue next to the appropriate word (a clock next to *hour*) to enable the test giver to distinguish the words. Once partners are selected, they select a place to work and follow this procedure:

1. Partners exchange lists and decide who will be quizzed first.
2. Quiz givers call out each word and use it in a sentence.
3. If the quiz giver can't read a word, he or she asks the teacher.
4. No hints are allowed except in the instance when the quiz giver can't read a word he or she may say "It's the only word on your list that begins with an a." Often the test taker will know the word and the test may proceed without asking the teacher for assistance.

5. Once the first quiz is finished, the partners switch roles. When both tests are complete, partners take the test to the teacher to check the test on the spot.

6. Words misspelled on the test are recycled into the spelling journal (WINK list).

If a student habitually scores poorly, confer with him or her to find out why. He or she may need to be more careful, work harder, or switch to a lower-level spelling list. Super spellers use spelling workshop for vocabulary enrichment and to identify words that they might use in their writing but aren't sure how to spell. Like other students in spelling workshop, they are developing word-specific knowledge at a level that matches their ability. (Gentry, October 1997, "Spelling Strategies," *Instructor*, New York: Scholastic, p. 77; and 2000)

Set a tone of high priority and high expectations for your spelling workshop. This important opportunity for fourth-, fifth-, and sixth-grade students to expand their word-specific knowledge will impact more than their writing, reading, and thinking. Knowledge of words impacts every aspect of learning.

CHAPTER 8

FOURTH-, FIFTH-, AND SIXTH-GRADE LITERACY MAPS

Sho Yano, a 10-year-old prodigy, is a college freshman at Loyola University in Chicago majoring in biology. At 10 years old, Sho is far beyond fourth-grade writing benchmarks. He wrote a comparative analysis of Al Gore and George W. Bush's prescription drug proposals for his freshman English composition class. (Davis, 2000) When Sho was kindergarten age, his parents recognized that he far exceeded normal kindergarten-level benchmarks. After all, Sho was reading and playing Chopin before age four. Sho's achievement during his elementary and middle school years was so extraordinary that his parents opted to home-school him during that time. They knew Sho was a genius. They knew him as an individual. They used this understanding to make sure that his special needs were met. In essence, they put Sho on the map that he needed—a map quite different than what might be expected for most children his age.

Some critics point to children like Sho and claim that grade-level standards are artificial. They make a point I agree with—all children are different. They argue that one cannot get an accurate portrait of an individual's literacy achievement based on standards because benchmarks don't acknowledge the true range in abilities in grades four through six. My contention is just the opposite: benchmarks help bring the true range of abilities into sharper focus. Benchmarks clarify what needs to be taught and to whom. A particular student's instructional needs, of course, may be above- or below-grade level. But using benchmarks as a marker of what is expected helps the teacher know the student individually and better meet his or her individual needs.

This chapter is about that process—knowing students individually and taking the steps to meet their individual needs. There are specific and concrete grade-level learning goals for literacy translated into grade-level benchmarks. The Benchmark Checklists on pages 147–161 are provided for you to reproduce and place in the front of each child's portfolio as an individual assessment for that child. The grade-level set of benchmarks is organized in clusters of the essential literacy elements: Listening Comprehension, Exposure to Print, Reading Comprehension and Fluency, Word-Specific Knowledge, Writing, Spelling, Ideas and World Knowledge, and Attitudes about Reading and Writing. The Benchmark Checklists assessment tool will help you know each student in your classroom as a literacy learner. (Additional benchmarks for Technology Literacy and for Poetry follow in Chapter 9.)

WHY USE GRADE-LEVEL BENCHMARKS?

It makes sense to use a map with grade-level benchmarks because our schools are organized in grade levels. These grade-level benchmarks must have developmental integrity, but they can be based on the fact that chronological age or grade level provides fairly accurate criteria for the minimal expectation of what should be happening with literacy development.

Benchmarks must be specific to each grade level. You should not have the same benchmark at one grade level that you have at the next, although some state curriculum standards documents confuse this issue. For example, contrast one state's fourth-grade benchmark for comprehension with its comparable fifth-grade benchmark:

READING/ENGLISH LANGUAGE ARTS–GRADE 4

I. Reading/Literature

B. **The student will read and demonstrate comprehension of a variety of literary forms to include fiction, nonfiction, biographies, and historical fiction.**
   - Explain the author's purpose
     (other bulleted items follow)

(Reading/English Language Arts, 1998, p. 11)

READING/ENGLISH LANGUAGE ARTS–GRADE 5

I. Reading/Literature

B. **The student will continue to read and demonstrate comprehension of a variety of literary forms to include fiction, nonfiction, and poetry.**
   - Describe character development in fiction and poetry selections
     (other bulleted items follow)

(Reading/English Language Arts, 1998, p. 15)

Statements I-B for grades four and five do not differentiate between a fourth-grade and fifth-grade level for comprehension of a variety of literary forms. While different bulleted items are presented under I-B for each grade level, the items do not differentiate fourth-grade-level comprehension from fifth-grade-level comprehension. In point of fact, both fourth-grade and fifth-grade readers would be expected to "Explain the author's purpose" and to "Describe character development in fiction and poetry selections." These state standards clearly do not identify a difference in comprehension at the fourth- and fifth-grade levels.

> Differentiation of what is expected at fourth versus fifth grade must be based on the difficulty of the text being read.

We assess comprehension the same way in fourth and fifth grade, but we have to assess it using different levels of text. The problem with the statements presented above is that they are not really benchmarks because they are not tied to specific levels of text. These vague standards are of little use. The statements can easily be revised into well-constructed benchmarks as follows: "Can the child comprehend *Little House in the Big Woods* by Laura Ingalls Wilder?" (an appropriate benchmark book for fourth grade) versus "Can the child comprehend *Bridge to Terabithia* by Katherine Paterson?" (an appropriate benchmark book for fifth grade). Chapter 4 provides an example of how the text becomes more complex at each grade level by contrasting a fourth-grade level text (*Beezus and Ramona* by Beverly Cleary) with a fifth-grade level text (*The Great Fire* by Jim Murphy).

BENCHMARKS ARE NOT ABOUT MEMORIZING FACTS

Those who do not understand the way standards relate to learning goals suggest that standards *should* be vague. Vague standards only make sense for world knowledge, such as accounting for when students should learn the names of explorers, state capitals, or the definition of a predicate. Exactly when a child should learn about the explorers or the fact that Raleigh is the capital of North Carolina is somewhat arbitrary. This kind of knowledge includes a very broad spectrum of topics and facts. Specificity of standards, however, does not equate to long lists of facts and skills that students must acquire.

The benchmarks in this book are learning goals for reading and comprehending text at a certain level, writing at a certain level of sophistication, or demonstrating a certain level of word-specific knowledge in correct spelling. You will see that the Benchmark Checklists for each grade level are relatively short and easy to use—only 40 questions for each of grades four, five, and six. These questions have nothing to do with long lists of dates or definitions that students ought to know at a particular grade level. Rather, they account for the minimal level of literacy functioning that is expected for each student at that grade level if the student is on track developmentally.

The Benchmark Checklists are tied to levels of sophistication of learning. The one exception is the benchmark for Attitudes about Reading and Writing. This essential literacy element restates the same benchmark questions year after year. Other benchmarks, such as those for Reading Comprehension, Spelling, and Writing change qualitatively each year by "raising the bar" as teachers assess for a higher level of performance each year. One never really "raises the bar" when assessing attitudes. The standards do not change when assessing attitudes; however, the student's attitude might change. A student who had good attitudes about reading and writing in fourth grade may develop poor ones in fifth grade. A student who had great attitudes in fifth grade may need new motivation in sixth grade. You must reassess attitude benchmarks each year. (Gentry, 2000a)

In assessing Attitudes about Reading and Writing, the teacher determines whether the child engages in stimulating and active performance as a reader and writer. Teachers have no difficulty assessing these benchmarks by observation when they know their students, make school useful and interesting, create reading/writing classrooms, and personalize instruction.

WHAT ABOUT INDIVIDUAL DIFFERENCES?

Grade-level standards take individual differences into account by helping you know the individual. The notion that grade-by-grade standards will result in willful disregard of individual differences is, in the long run, patently false. Of course students develop at different rates. But minimal acceptable literacy standards take into account the fact that under optimal conditions students may perform far beyond what is expected. Under restrictive conditions—really poor teaching, time wasted in school, or inappropriate curricula—students may perform below what is expected. Under reasonable conditions, however, we can be fairly specific about what is expected. The specificity of the Benchmark Checklists make it easier for you to know each student in your classroom as a reader, writer, speller, user of words, and a thinker. Assessment and instruction must match the child in order for that child to perform at his or her best.

BENCHMARKS MAKE ASSESSMENT EASIER

It is appropriate to think of assessment as an ongoing part of everyday activity in the classroom. You sit down with students on a daily basis not only to teach but also to figure out how successful they have been. Ongoing assessment is continuous, with ample opportunities to judge what is happening. The more samples taken, the more accurate the assessment is likely to be. No reading test can judge a student's reading comprehension better than a well-trained, competent teacher who has worked with the student for an entire year, observing the child daily, individually, and in small groups, as a thoughtful, responsive reader. Tests may add to teacher assessments but the best methods of assessments are recording observations of children as readers, writers, thinkers, and word users.

School administrators should aim for a closer connection among assessment, curriculum, and instruction. The idea of "teaching to the test" is a problem only when the test is inappropriate. If assessments are appropriate measures of how effectively students are learning to use literacy to think and explore ideas, we should teach to the test! Real assessment happens when teachers choose appropriate evaluations and learning goals for each student in the classroom.

BENCHMARKS EMPOWER TEACHERS

What if you taught in one of the nation's largest school systems where most students score well-below grade level in reading and math? What if standardized tests were the only measure of your success as a teacher regardless of where students were functioning when they entered your classroom in the fall? What if the media continually reported that something had to be done because "results show schools remain in deep distress?" You might feel that things were out of your control. Benchmarks allow you to experience a feeling of control in your classroom and accountability for your students' learning.

If you have wondered how to offset the fear of being "graded" as a school or a teacher by high stakes testing, the answer is to demonstrate what you are accomplishing. Benchmarks allow you to prove where students were functioning when they came to you and where they function when they leave. "When she came to me, she was reading and comprehending this book on this level and her writing looked like this. Now she reads on this level and her writing looks like this." Benchmarks provide the proof! If students come to your fifth-grade classroom functioning at a second-grade level, no one can fault you when they leave your classroom functioning below fifth-grade level on a standardized test. Without benchmarks it may be hard to prove the progress students have actually made due to your teaching.

HOW THE BENCHMARK ASSESSMENT WORKS

Your assessment begins with a careful analysis of the student's writing to determine indicators for as many of the benchmark questions as possible. Assessing writing first makes sense because so many of the underlying knowledge sources for literacy are displayed in student writing. If we know what to look for, student writing may show us both soft and hard evidence of literacy development. It not only shows how the student is functioning as a writer, but reveals the literacy devices the child is using as a reader, a speller, a thinker, a speaker, and a listener. A student's writing is a footprint of how he or she uses words and underlying knowledge sources such as phonics. Writing gives evidence of how the student uses literacy devices learned from listening and reading. One can even get "soft signs" of the way the student processes as a reader by observing the devices and techniques he or she uses in writing. Wide reading predicts good writing. Likewise, the best writers in grades four through six are often the best readers because a child's writing improves in almost every aspect from wide reading.

Spelling doesn't automatically get perfect with wide reading and writing just as children don't "catch" perfect spelling by reading and writing (Peters, 1985); nevertheless, there certainly are connections. A teacher can easily monitor some aspects of spelling development by looking at a writing sample. He or she may assess phonics development and vocabulary development by checking writing.

Too often, ongoing classroom assessment gets short shrift. Its power is that it is continuous. Its reliability and validity lie in the fact that the more samples you take in authentic contexts, the more likely you are to get an accurate picture of the individual. Ongoing assessment gives you volumes of evidence of each child's literacy growth, yet it is easy to do because there are only a few specific and concrete benchmarks to assess. Your everyday opportunities to observe students make ongoing assessment seem effortless. Quite simply, the grade-level Benchmark Checklists help you observe students with a purpose. Follow these steps in your benchmark assessment:

STEP ONE: Study a writing sample for information relevant to the grade-level benchmarks. Ask the child to read the writing sample aloud. You may wish to ask questions about the sample to find out more about each benchmark under consideration. Assess as many of the benchmarks as possible from the child's writing. Answer the remaining benchmark questions through ongoing classroom assessment.

STEP TWO: Go through each remaining benchmark, considering the essential literacy areas: Listening Comprehension, Exposure to Print, Reading Comprehension and Fluency, Word-Specific Knowledge, Writing, Spelling, Ideas and World Knowledge, Attitudes about Reading and Writing. Much of the assessment of the child's progress on these remaining benchmarks can be done by observation in the context of daily classroom activity.

Become intimately familiar with the Benchmark Checklist for your grade level. Think of it as your map. Allow it to help you know the particulars of each student's literacy functioning and allow this information to guide your teaching. Keep in mind that you must match students with the map that is appropriate for their levels of functioning. If a child is functioning below- or above-grade level in certain areas, you must match that child with appropriate benchmarks for his or her level of functioning. Suggestions for working with students whose level of functioning are below fourth-grade level are provided in Chapter 2.

Think of each day in your classroom as an opportunity to collect the evidence you need to assess each child's functioning in each of the important benchmark areas and to provide appropriate instruction. Remember, the more samples of literacy taken in authentic contexts the more likely you are to get an accurate picture of each individual and meet the student's instructional needs.

BENCHMARK CHECKLISTS

The Benchmark Checklists on the following pages are provided for you to reproduce and place in the front of each child's portfolio as an individual assessment for that child.

Conduct ongoing benchmark checks for each child. I recommend conducting formal benchmark checks in September, January, and May. These checks allow you to monitor each child and the effectiveness of your teaching.

- The purpose of the **September Baseline Benchmark Check** is to find out where each child is functioning at the start of the school year and establish starting points of instruction.
- The **January Benchmark Check** is the midyear check to determine which benchmarks each child has achieved and those to strive for during the remaining months of the school year. The midyear

check allows you to plan, teach, and assess more efficiently and effectively for the remainder of the year.

- The **May Benchmark Check** allows you to be accountable for each child's literacy growth during the time he or she has been in your classroom. It allows you to track each individual's growth and to record specific achievement in light of the goals you set in September.

Use the same checklist for September, January, and May, recording the dates beside your observation of whether a particular benchmark was "Not Yet" met, "Some/Sometimes" met, or "All/Always" met. At the end of the year, you will not only verify that a child has reached a particular benchmark, but you will know where that child was at the beginning of the year with that benchmark, how progress toward reaching the benchmark developed, and when the benchmark was finally met.

FOURTH-GRADE BENCHMARK CHECKLIST

NAME: _____

AGE: _____

TEACHER: _____

Record the date in the appropriate box for each question. Comment or give examples in the spaces provided.

LISTENING COMPREHENSION	Not Yet	Some/Sometimes	All/Always
4-1. Listens and comprehends appropriate content material designed for grade four			

EXPOSURE TO PRINT	Not Yet	Some/Sometimes	All/Always
4-2. Reads extensively, fostering listening comprehension, conceptual understandings, vocabulary, and world knowledge appropriate for grade four			
4-3. Reads fairly lengthy chapter books appropriate for grade four			
4-4. Selects and reads trade books appropriate for grade four			

READING COMPREHENSION AND FLUENCY	Not Yet	Some/Sometimes	All/Always
4-5. Reads aloud with fluency and comprehension any text that is appropriately designed for the first half of grade four			
4-6. Reads and comprehends both fiction and nonfiction text that is appropriately designed for the second half of grade four			
4-7. Predicts and justifies what will happen next in stories appropriate for grade four			
4-8. Discusses *how*, *who*, and *what* if questions in nonfiction text appropriate for grade four			
4-9. Discusses similarities in characters and events across stories appropriate for grade four			

READING COMPREHENSION AND FLUENCY	Not Yet	Some/Sometimes	All/Always
4-10. In interpreting fiction, discusses underlying theme or message in material appropriate for grade four			
4-11. In interpreting nonfiction, distinguishes cause and effect, fact and opinion, main idea and supporting details in material appropriate for grade four			
4-12. Uses multiple resources to locate information in material appropriate for grade four (e.g., table of contents, index, available technology)			

WORD-SPECIFIC KNOWLEDGE	Not Yet	Some/Sometimes	All/Always
4-13. Increases sight word recognition to include fourth-grade level words			
4-14. Spells correctly a collection of fourth-grade level spelling words			
4-15. Extends accuracy in reading and understanding fourth-grade level vocabulary			
4-16. Infers word meaning from taught roots, prefixes, and suffixes in material appropriate for grade four			
4-17. Uses new vocabulary in speech and writing			

WRITING	Not Yet	Some/Sometimes	All/Always
4-18. Produces longer compositions appropriate for grade four (See fourth-grade model on page 162.)			
4-19. Demonstrates concrete thinking when writing, such as following a story map in a specific, clear-cut, step-by-step sequence; pictures events mentally and writes about them concretely though detail may not be always apparent			

WRITING	Not Yet	Some/Sometimes	All/Always
4-20. Begins to write in paragraph form though paragraphing may not be fully understood; paragraphing is sometimes uneven and random			
4-21. Indents and punctuates for dialogue with correctness (This is an end of fourth-grade benchmark.)			
4-22. Independently reviews work for mechanics with age-appropriate success			
4-23. Independently reviews work for spelling; locates and corrects virtually all misspelled words in independent writing (NOTE: Writers who spell below fourth-grade level need editorial support in reaching benchmark 4-23. Expect these spellers to demonstrate a habit of coming to the teacher to get needed support. This practice teaches spelling consciousness and good spelling habits.)			
4-24. Uses formal language patterns in his or her own writing including literate syntax and vocabulary appropriate for grade four			
4-25. Continues to use prewriting, drafting, revision, and editing processes in producing compositions and reports (Note: This is an end of third-grade benchmark; reassess for continued use. Prewriting tends to receive more focus in third grade; revising more in fourth grade.)			
4-26. Continues to use a variety of formal sentence structures in his or her writing (Note: This is a third-grade benchmark. Check for more sophisticated sentence structure appropriate for grade four.)			
SPELLING	Not Yet	Some/Sometimes	All/Always
4-27. Spells correctly an increasing number of fourth-grade level words			

SPELLING	Not Yet	Some/Sometimes	All/Always
4-28. Finds virtually all misspelled words in writing			
4-29. Spells correctly previously studied fourth-grade level words and spelling patterns in his/her writing			
4-30. Uses the dictionary and other resources to check and correct unknown spelling in writing			

IDEAS AND WORLD KNOWLEDGE	Not Yet	Some/Sometimes	All/Always
4-31. Expresses ideas, thinks creatively, and organizes information in ways that are appropriate for grade four			
4-32. Demonstrates age-appropriate world knowledge, expanding ideas and vocabulary			

ATTITUDES ABOUT READING AND WRITING	Not Yet	Some/Sometimes	All/Always
4-33. Chooses to read independently Comment or give examples:			
4-34. Chooses to write independently Comment or give examples:			
4-35. Chooses to read in a sustained way for a period of time Comment or give examples:			

ATTITUDES ABOUT READING AND WRITING	Not Yet	Some/Sometimes	All/Always
4-36. Chooses to write in a sustained way for a period of time			

Comment or give examples:

_____

_____

_____

_____

4-37. Chooses reading-related activities for enjoyment			

Comment or give examples:

_____

_____

_____

_____

4-38. Chooses writing-related activities for enjoyment			

Comment or give examples:

_____

_____

_____

_____

4-39. Chooses to read both fiction and nonfiction			

Comment or give examples:

_____

_____

_____

_____

4-40. Chooses to write both fiction and nonfiction			

Comment or give examples:

_____

_____

_____

_____

FIFTH-GRADE BENCHMARK CHECKLIST

NAME: _____

AGE: _____

TEACHER: _____

Record the date in the appropriate box for each question. Comment or give examples in the spaces provided.

LISTENING COMPREHENSION	Not Yet	Some/Sometimes	All/Always
5-1. Listens and comprehends appropriate content material designed for grade five			

EXPOSURE TO PRINT	Not Yet	Some/Sometimes	All/Always
5-2. Reads extensively, fostering listening comprehension, conceptual understandings, vocabulary, and world knowledge appropriate for grade five			
5-3. Reads fairly lengthy chapter books appropriate for grade five			
5-4. Selects and reads trade books appropriate for grade five			

READING COMPREHENSION AND FLUENCY	Not Yet	Some/Sometimes	All/Always
5-5. Reads aloud with fluency and comprehension any text that is appropriately designed for the first half of grade five			
5-6. Reads and comprehends both fiction and nonfiction text that is appropriately designed for the second half of grade five			
5-7. Predicts and justifies what will happen next in stories appropriate for grade five			
5-8. Discusses *how*, *who*, and *what* if questions in nonfiction text appropriate for grade five			
5-9. Discusses similarities in characters and events across stories appropriate for grade five			

READING COMPREHENSION AND FLUENCY	Not Yet	Some/Sometimes	All/Always
5-10. In interpreting fiction, discusses underlying theme or message in material appropriate for grade five			
5-11. In interpreting nonfiction, distinguishes cause and effect, fact and opinion, main idea and supporting details in material appropriate for grade five			
5-12. Uses multiple resources to locate information in material appropriate for grade five (e.g., table of contents, index, available technology)			

WORD-SPECIFIC KNOWLEDGE	Not Yet	Some/Sometimes	All/Always
5-13. Increases sight word recognition to include fifth-grade level words			
5-14. Spells correctly a collection of fifth-grade level spelling words			
5-15. Extends accuracy in reading and understanding fifth-grade level vocabulary			
5-16. Infers word meaning from taught roots, prefixes, and suffixes in material appropriate for grade five			
5-17. Uses new vocabulary in speech and writing			

WRITING	Not Yet	Some/Sometimes	All/Always
5-18. Produces longer compositions appropriate for grade five (See fifth-grade model on page 163.)			
5-19. Demonstrates abstract thinking in writing; may apply known or experienced information to new situations in writing			
5-20. Paragraphing comes naturally			

WRITING	Not Yet	Some/Sometimes	All/Always
5-21. Begins to use transitions when writing several paragraphs though not with great sophistication			
5-22. Independently reviews work for mechanics with age-appropriate success			
5-23. Independently reviews work for spelling; locates and corrects virtually all misspelled words in independent writing. (NOTE: Writers who spell below fifth-grade level need editorial support in reaching benchmark 5-23. Expect these spellers to demonstrate a habit of coming to the teacher to get needed support. This practice teaches spelling consciousness and good spelling habits.)			
5-24. Uses formal language patterns in his or her own writing, including literate syntax and vocabulary appropriate for grade five			
5-25. Continues to use all writing steps in producing compositions and reports; however, direction and focus may come during the drafting. Stages of the writing process are integrated, reciprocal, recursive, and less distinct			
5-26. Continues to use a variety of formal sentence structures in his or her writing. (Note: This is a third- and fourth-grade benchmark. Check for more sophisticated sentence structure appropriate for grade five.)			

SPELLING	Not Yet	Some/Sometimes	All/Always
5-27. Spells correctly an increasing number of fifth-grade level words			
5-28. Finds virtually all misspelled words in writing			
5-29. Spells correctly previously studied fifth-grade level words and spelling patterns in his or her writing			

Fifth-Grade Benchmarks

SPELLING	Not Yet	Some/Sometimes	All/Always
5-30. Uses the dictionary and other resources to check and correct unknown spelling in writing			

IDEAS AND WORLD KNOWLEDGE	Not Yet	Some/Sometimes	All/Always
5-31. Expresses ideas, thinks creatively, and organizes information in ways that are appropriate for grade five			
5-32. Demonstrates age-appropriate world knowledge, expanding ideas and vocabulary			

ATTITUDES ABOUT READING AND WRITING	Not Yet	Some/Sometimes	All/Always
5-33. Chooses to read independently			

Comment or give examples:

_____

_____

_____

_____

5-34. Chooses to write independently			

Comment or give examples:

_____

_____

_____

5-35. Chooses to read in a sustained way for a period of time			

Comment or give examples:

_____

_____

_____

5-36. Chooses to write in a sustained way for a period of time			

Comment or give examples:

_____

_____

_____

ATTITUDES ABOUT READING AND WRITING	Not Yet	Some/Sometimes	All/Always
5-37. Chooses reading-related activities for enjoyment			

Comment or give examples:

_____

_____

_____

_____

5-38. Chooses writing-related activities for enjoyment			

Comment or give examples:

_____

_____

_____

_____

5-39. Chooses to read both fiction and nonfiction			

Comment or give examples:

_____

_____

_____

_____

5-40. Chooses to write both fiction and nonfiction			

Comment or give examples:

_____

_____

_____

_____

SIXTH-GRADE BENCHMARK CHECKLIST

NAME: _____

AGE: _____

TEACHER: _____

Record the date in the appropriate box for each question. Comment or give examples in the spaces provided.

LISTENING COMPREHENSION	Not Yet	Some/Sometimes	All/Always
6-1. Listens and comprehends appropriate content material designed for grade six			

EXPOSURE TO PRINT	Not Yet	Some/Sometimes	All/Always
6-2. Reads extensively, fostering listening comprehension, conceptual understandings, vocabulary, and world knowledge appropriate for grade six			
6-3. Reads fairly lengthy chapter books appropriate for grade six			
6-4. Selects and reads trade books appropriate for grade six			

READING COMPREHENSION AND FLUENCY	Not Yet	Some/Sometimes	All/Always
6-5. Reads aloud with fluency and comprehension any text that is appropriately designed for the first half of grade six			
6-6. Reads and comprehends both fiction and nonfiction text that is appropriately designed for the second half of grade six			
6-7. Predicts and justifies what will happen next in stories appropriate for grade six			
6-8. Discusses *how*, *who*, and *what* if questions in nonfiction text appropriate for grade six			
6-9. Discusses similarities in characters and events across stories appropriate for grade six			

READING COMPREHENSION AND FLUENCY	Not Yet	Some/Sometimes	All/Always
6-10. In interpreting fiction, discusses under-lying theme or message in material appropriate for grade six			
6-11. In interpreting nonfiction, distinguishes cause and effect, fact and opinion, main idea and supporting details in material appropriate for grade six			
6-12. Uses multiple resources to locate informa-tion in material appropriate for grade six (e.g., table of contents, index, available technology)			

WORD-SPECIFIC KNOWLEDGE	Not Yet	Some/Sometimes	All/Always
6-13. Increases sight word recognition to include sixth-grade level words			
6-14. Spells correctly a collection of sixth-grade level spelling words			
6-15. Extends accuracy in reading and under-standing sixth-grade level vocabulary			
6-16. Infers word meaning from taught roots, prefixes, and suffixes in material appropriate for grade six			
6-17. Uses new vocabulary in speech and writing			

WRITING	Not Yet	Some/Sometimes	All/Always
6-18. Produces longer compositions appropriate for grade six (See sixth-grade model on page 165.)			
6-19. Begins to write with voice more naturally			
6-20. Uses transition with variation and sophistication when writing several paragraphs			
6-21. Prewriting, drafting, revision, and editing processes in producing compositions and reports tend to be ongoing, reciprocal, and recursive with no clear-cut lines between them; these processes are often simultaneous with drafting			

WRITING	Not Yet	Some/Sometimes	All/Always
6-22. Continues to use a variety of formal sentence structures in his or her writing; writing reflects age-appropriate world knowledge and thinking			
6-23. Assimilates information into abstract schemes, tests own hypotheses as a writer, thinks about his or her own thinking while writing			
6-24. Demonstrates more abstract thinking as a writer and continues to demonstrate even more knowledge about what constitutes good writing and more independence in thinking			
6-25. Uses formal language patterns in his or her own writing including literate syntax and vocabulary appropriate for grade six			
6-26. Independently reviews work for spelling and mechanics as a courtesy to the reader			

SPELLING	Not Yet	Some/Sometimes	All/Always
6-27. Spells correctly an increasing number of sixth-grade level words			
6-28. Finds virtually all misspelled words in writing			
6-29. Spells correctly previously studied sixth-grade level words and spelling patterns in his or her writing			
6-30. Uses the dictionary and other resources to check and correct unknown spelling in writing			

IDEAS AND WORLD KNOWLEDGE	Not Yet	Some/Sometimes	All/Always
6-31. Expresses ideas, thinks creatively, and organizes information in ways that are appropriate for grade six			
6-32. Demonstrates age-appropriate world knowledge, expanding ideas and vocabulary			

ATTITUDES ABOUT READING AND WRITING	Not Yet	Some/Sometimes	All/Always
6-33. Chooses to read independently			
Comment or give examples:			

6-34. Chooses to write independently

Comment or give examples:

6-35. Chooses to read in a sustained way for a period of time

Comment or give examples:

6-36. Chooses to write in a sustained way for a period of time

Comment or give examples:

6-37. Chooses reading-related activities for enjoyment

Comment or give examples:

ATTITUDES ABOUT READING AND WRITING	Not Yet	Some/Sometimes	All/Always
6-38. Chooses writing-related activities for enjoyment			

Comment or give examples:

_____

_____

_____

_____

	Not Yet	Some/Sometimes	All/Always
6-39. Chooses to read both fiction and nonfiction			

Comment or give examples:

_____

_____

_____

_____

	Not Yet	Some/Sometimes	All/Always
6-40. Chooses to write both fiction and nonfiction			

Comment or give examples:

_____

_____

_____

_____

GRADE-LEVEL WRITING SAMPLES

FOURTH-GRADE SAMPLE: THE DECISION
(CHAPTER 1 OF A LONGER PIECE)

Deep in the forest lived families of bugs and rodents. One particular family of mice lived in a small hut in between roots and leaves. This family had a mother, a father, and a small mouse called Annie. Annie was a very brave mouse and had lots of friends. Many of them had families like hers, like the rats, the cockroaches, the mayflies, the ladybugs, and the lightning bugs. One afternoon Kristy Mayfly, Ralph Rat, Lila and Luke Lady Bug, Clarence Cockroach, Willie Worm, Ed Lightning Bug, and Annie were meeting in their clubhouse and Luke said, "We should go away."

"What do you mean go away?" Ed demanded.

"Well, I don't know about you, but my house isn't very fun any more," Luke explained.

"I know what you mean, " Ralph said.

"Last week my mom gave all my good toys to that baby fly that just hatched, and we've been having the same meal for weeks!"

"Yeh! The same things have been happening to me!" Lila said.

"Well, you decide Annie. You are the club president," Luke said.

"I think we should go," Annie decided, "and we should pack right now!"

CHARACTERISTICS OF FOURTH-GRADE WRITING

- Easily constructed stories and narratives
- Step-by-step sequence
- Narratives follow a chain of events and a chronology that the writer can go back and experience
- Equal attention to each story event
- Story maps followed deliberately
- Draft written straight through; little shifting of focus between reading and writing the draft
- Single focus within a piece
- Abundance of dialogue in stories and narratives
- Few complex transitions
- Revision concrete, focusing on correct spelling, capitalization, punctuation, and attention to the question: "Does it sound right?"
- Paragraphing evident but sometimes uneven and random
- Dialogue indented and punctuated

FIFTH-GRADE SAMPLE: CAMPING ON AN ISLAND

Camping on an island in Maine is one of my favorite things to do. Walking on the beaches, toasting marshmallows and looking for Pirate's Treasure are just a few of the fun things my family and I do!

When we get there, the first thing we do is choose a campsite. It's really fun because there're so many different ones. My favorite site is #9 on the harbor side. There's a huge climbing tree and a trail that leads to the rocks and the beach which makes things even more cool. Picking a site may seem dull, but it's really fun! After we put our tent up we go walk on the beach. It's nice to stretch our legs after the long car ride.

There's a log on one of the beaches that my brother, Matty and I play on. I love seeing the sunset from the beach before dinner. I enjoy the beaches on the island. They're really cool.

When it gets dark out after dinner we roast marshmallows. I like mine golden brown, but my dad likes them black (yuck!). It's nice to sit by the fire with a stomach full of marshmallows!

The next morning we get up early and hike on some of the trails. Lots of the trails are loops but some go places, like the trail to Crescent Beach! Sometimes you don't know where you'll end up.

Going on Crescent Beach is fun because I know when I get there it's going to be really cool! There are tide pools with some really cool creatures and seaweed in them! But my favorite thing about it, even though we go in spring or fall, is it is usually warm enough to get a little wet. I always look forward to going there.

Another fun thing to do is to go kayaking. It's really awesome! One time we went out to a couple of islands. It's not hard work and you can explore neat places. Once, before we went kayaking my brother and I found Pirate's treasure! Of course, it wasn't really Pirate treasure, but it was still money! We split it in half.

No matter what you do when you camp on an island, you're bound to have tons of fun!

CHARACTERISTICS OF FIFTH-GRADE WRITING

- Writing more abstract than in fourth grade—may not reveal a step-by-step process
- Direction and focus may change during the drafting
- Possible lack of clear-cut line between prewriting, drafting, editing, and revision; each may be reciprocal, recursive, and ongoing during the drafting
- Natural paragraphing

- Use of transitions when writing several paragraphs though not with ease and sophistication
- Increasing knowledge about what constitutes good writing; more polish and sophistication, especially in revising
- Revision beyond what is concrete (e.g., increased sophistication in revising leads and transitions as opposed to only focusing on correct spelling and punctuation)
- Prewriting and planning ahead more sophisticated
- Reflection upon the content of the writing via his or her own thinking
- Abstractly applies knowledge and experiences to new situations
- Reflects more abstraction in thought: complex problem solving, discovery of alternative routes, testing and confirming hypotheses, going from specific observations to broad generalizations
- May roam, discover, and invent beyond the bounds of the original story map
- Ease with inclusion of elaboration and detail
- Shifts beyond a single focus within a single piece

SIXTH-GRADE SAMPLE: JULY 3RD—GETTYSBURG

July 3rd—Gettysburg

As I stood there with all the men standing in a line as far as I could see I thought, "If this is the last time I breathe then so be it." But really even though I put on a good face I couldn't help wondering if I would ever see my home again or taste Ma's quince pie. How I wished I could just disappear right then and there.

I thought back to the first battle in Manassas, how scared I had been and I must admit I thought I'd be brave at a moment like this, like I was at previous battles.

I looked way up at Seminary Ridge where Yankee cannons were pointing down at me. I saw the round tops with more cannons, but most of all I saw the long rolling wheat fields ahead and that was what scared me; not the cannons or the Union soldiers behind the big stone wall. I wondered if the Billy Yanks could see my knees trembling or how my gun quavered in my shaking hands.

I recalled one day, Lee had said, "It is a fine thing war is so horrible for otherwise a man could get to love it." I didn't agree with him then and I still don't now. If we could get to love war, then can't we love peace?

CHARACTERISTICS OF SIXTH-GRADE WRITING

- May reach high levels of sophistication
- Includes lots of detail even in the first draft
- Varies beginnings, endings, and transitions
- Weaves dialogue in naturally
- Allows the writer's voice to come through
- Brings voice to nonfiction
- Allows prewriting, editing, and revision to occur naturally and recursively
- Is free from distractions due to problems with spelling, punctuation, and conventions

TECHNOLOGY AND POETRY IN THE CLASSROOM

E-TEACHING

Log on-line and interface.
Find the perfect site.
E-mail —
Telecommunicate—
Upgrade your megabite
Use cross-modal linkages.
Now search the World Wide Web.
Digital technology
Is not about to ebb.

This tool expanding reasoning
May stretch a young child's mind
To new frontiers of learning
That impact all mankind.

Computers should not scare you—
Embrace this way to learn.
Your classroom's had the chalkboard—
Let computers have a turn!

J. Richard Gentry

This chapter juxtaposes technology and poetry because both have great promise to expand children's thinking and empower them to communicate more effectively. In many ways, literacy is like language itself—a complex, changing synergism of the past and the present. For me, the quintessential classrooms of the new millennium evoke images of new technology alongside what teachers have found enduring. Literacy benchmarks for fourth-, fifth-, and sixth-grade classrooms must include new uses of technology and a revival of a 4,500 year-old tradition of poetry.

TECHNOLOGY IN YOUR CLASSROOM

Are computers interfacing with the minds of children and changing the way children think? Are computers enhancing the way students find information, process words, and communicate with others? Is technology the stand-in for human interaction?

In some schools computers are already as much a part of the classroom as chalkboards. On February 15, 1998, when President Clinton and Vice President Gore announced the Technology Literacy Challenge, the U.S. government went public with a vision of a 21st century in which all students are technologically literate. Under this challenge, private citizens, parents, and the business community will join local, state, and federal governments to meet four national goals:

1. All teachers in the nation will have the training and support they need to help students learn to use computers and the information superhighway.
2. All teachers and students will have modern multimedia computers in their classrooms.
3. Every classroom will be connected to the information superhighway.
4. Effective software and on-line learning resources will be an integral part of every school's curriculum.

(Getting America's Students Ready for the 21st Century—Meeting the Technology Literacy Challenge: a Report to the Nation on Technology and Education from the United States Department of Education. June 29, 1996. *http://www.ed.gov/Technology/plan/Nat TechPlan/*)

With the prospect that computers will become commonplace in American classrooms, fourth-, fifth-, and sixth-grade teachers have joined the ranks of those who are trying to figure out how best to use digital technology. How should your fourth, fifth, and sixth graders be using computers? Jane M. Healy, author of *Failure to Connect: How Computers Affect Our Children's Minds—and What We Can Do About It* (1998) suggests age 10 as a good time to start "multimedia applications, research skills, and manipulating databases or spreadsheets. It is a good time for quality software to review the basics and fill in missing pieces, such as practicing spelling patterns and math 'facts.'" (p. 266)

At the same time, Healy points out that cross-modal linkages, such as imaging visuals while reading a text, focusing on text screens when there are buttons to click on, and operations that require reasoning about several things at one time, are hard work for some students in the intermediate grades. The same mental operations that restrict and define what fourth, fifth, and sixth graders can do as writers (see Chapter 5) set parameters and place certain limits on digital learning.

Computers in fourth-, fifth- and sixth-grade classrooms provide students with access to sources of information that have not been available previously. A child in an elementary school can now research any topic by going no further than his or her fingertips. The child can use computers to instantly communicate with other children in faraway places or to communicate with adults, including experts in areas of interest or authors they are reading. Additionally, computers have revolutionized the writing process. Word processing, editing tools, such as spell check, and the capacity for publishing extend far beyond pencil and paper.

In addition to practical classroom uses for computers, evidence is growing that computers, when used correctly, may be linked to gains in test scores. Professor Dale Mann of Teachers College, Professor Charol Shakeshaft of Hofstra University, and a team of Columbia University researchers conducted a 10-year study on the effectiveness of using technology when learning math, reading, and language arts skills. This study, conducted in West Virginia, showed achievement gains from a statewide comprehensive instructional technology program that began with the kindergarten class of 1990-1991. Hardware and software gave all students easy and regular access to a program that focused on the state's basic skills goals in reading, language arts, and mathematics. Professional development was also provided for teachers. Both quantitative and qualitative data were collected on the 1996-1997 fifth graders, the first cohort to have the benefit of the comprehensive instructional technology program over their entire school experience. Student achievement improved dramatically, and findings indicate that as much as 11% of the total variance in the basic skills achievement gain scores of fifth-grade students could be attributed to the technology program (Mann, Shakeshaft, Becker, and Kottkamp, 1999). The positive effects of the research of the West Virginia project continue to be impressive.

As a teacher in grades four, five, or six, consider these three questions as you think about the role of computers in your classroom:

1. How can technology be used effectively?
2. Is it possible that computers will "dumb down" your students?
3. What are the technology literacy benchmarks for each grade level?

HOW CAN TECHNOLOGY BE USED EFFECTIVELY IN YOUR CLASSROOM?

Let's consider five ways your students may use technology. Both in and out of the classroom, students use technology for:

- Finding information
- Word processing
- Communicating with others on-line
- Creating multimedia reports
- Playing games for entertainment

FINDING INFORMATION

Without question the World Wide Web provides powerful new ways for students in your classroom to find information. For example, I see sixth-grade boys using computers to become experts on fishing, a topic they are passionate about. I see sixth-grade girls researching their favorite women's soccer team. Their searches on the Web lead to all kinds of authentic expressions of literacy. They may interview experts or find print resources that allow them to combine the information superhighway with print. Using technology to find information has become a mainstay for fourth, fifth, and sixth graders. Along with this, teachers face a new set of challenges.

The information superhighway leads to the information flea market. Your students may now have unlimited sources of information at their fingertips, but that presents them with new demands and responsibilities. They must know how to use, reference, and evaluate information appropriately. Students must sort fact from opinion, and opinion from propaganda. They must compare, contrast, and think critically about information sources and the information that is being used. Plagiarism becomes a considerable issue. "Information literacy" must be separated from "information overload" in which too much information ruins a fifth-grade literacy project or a potentially creative piece of writing.

Concrete thinkers at the fourth-grade level may be especially vulnerable to being overwhelmed by which information to use when researching a project. A simple cut and paste job may give a false impression—to the teacher, the parent, or the student—that deep learning has occurred when, in fact, very little real understanding occurred. It's easy to cut and paste together scraps of information with no real purpose, synthesis, or learning. Teachers must be ready to model and reinforce the critical thinking strategies that are required for students to successfully navigate the information superhighway.

WORD PROCESSING

Over 20 years ago I was a struggling assistant professor at a "publish or perish" university. Computers were just coming onto the scene and, as you might imagine, many university professors were jumping on the technology bandwagon. Being a life-long technology klutz, I was one of the last to consider signing up for the computer course being offered for our department. "Gentry, you had better sign up and learn to write on the computer. It's 'publish or perish,' you know. The faculty who learn to write on the computer are the ones who will be getting out the most publications. If you want to get ahead, you had better sign up for that course!" I stubbornly refused because I didn't have time for it. If I was going to get articles published that semester, I reasoned to myself, I needed to spend my time reading, thinking, and writing—not taking a bunch of computer courses. Eventually my strategy paid off. I was one of the few who published, though those colleagues who "perished" left the university with outstanding word-processing skills.

The essence of writing is about sending a message. Writing is all about communicating ideas, not about technology. I eventually learned to use the computer by trial and error and now I can't imagine trying to get along without it. Sometimes I regret that I never took a computer course. But I've never had any confusion about one issue: computers aren't going to do the writing for you. All of those worthwhile ideas have to come from your brain.

Technology in the classroom is in its infancy. This became clear when I reviewed available literature on the subject. I found more issues than definitive answers. Are students better off receiving direct instruction in computer skills or learning the technology through demonstration, coaching, and independent exploration as they use the computer? I can't tell you when and how best to teach students to write on a keyboard, but it is obvious that some structure for learning keyboarding makes sense. No one seems to know the exact effects of learning and using software tools, such as the spell-check. As a weak speller myself, I am sure spell-check is a good thing for everybody. It makes writing with perfect spelling easier for fourth, fifth, and sixth graders and reinforces good spelling habits.

Eventually, questions regarding how best to use computers for word processing in and out of the classroom will be resolved. As a teacher, it makes sense to recognize the practical benefits of word processing and to expect your students to acquire some skill in understanding and using the technology.

COMMUNICATING WITH OTHERS ON-LINE

There are many opportunities for your students to use E-mail, tele-conferencing, and other forms of technology to communicate with others.

Technology makes it possible to find new ways to take advantage of the social context of learning.

The purpose of literacy is to communicate with others. E-mail and telecommunications bring a whole new dimension to literacy learning. Remember when you were in elementary school, how it was more fun to write to a pen pal than to write a letter as an assignment? Authentic communication, such as E-mailing a student in Japan or Turkey, is inherently interesting and has great potential for posing new questions (What are other people's lives like? How are they like me? How are they different from me?) for genuine learning. Having students send E-mails from your classroom (copied to the teacher) increases a child's volume of writing. However, when opening up venues for E-mailing in your classroom, always ask: What learning is happening?

In some ways, using computers to communicate with others is like using integrated thematic units. The focus should remain on the desired learning outcomes or literacy benchmarks that are supposed to be accomplished. The teacher who loves to have students E-mail students in another country may be like the teacher who loves to study penguins every year. He or she may be convinced that the learning is somehow deeper, more authentic, broader, and more meaningful because it's couched in a thematic unit. Tim Shanahan's research showed the fallacy of that belief. He was unable to identify a study in any field with any age level that "clearly demonstrated more coherent or deeper understandings, or better applicability of learning as a result of integration" (Shanahan, 1997, p. 15). The notion of integrated thematic units is a great idea as long as it's tied to literacy benchmarks. The same thing may be said about communicating via computers. The computer must be used to achieve literacy benchmarks. There is no great benefit in having children spend a lot of time E-mailing if no learning is happening.

CREATING MULTIMEDIA REPORTS

Multimedia reports are effective ways for students to communicate their ideas. However, multimedia is not a replacement for reading, writing, listening, or speaking. Three important questions surrounding multimedia reports are:

1) When should students start using multimedia?
2) How should this technology be introduced?
3) Does the multimedia assignment help the student think more deeply, organize information more effectively, or elaborate a topic more thoroughly?

Carol Baroudi, author of *Internet for Dummies* suggests age 11 as "an optimal age for introduction to electronic communications" (Reported in

Healy, p. 250). In *Failure to Connect*, Healy tells about an experience meeting a 12-year-old in a suburban school who presented a multimedia report on King Tut. The child "arranged the setup to run on a large liquid crystal display screen mounted on the wall" (p. 148). The presentation included background music, maps, and his recorded voice reading a script he had written. A screen appeared for topics, such as "history," "geography," and "tomb artifacts" and icons allowed the viewer to control how the material would be presented. The presentation included slide shows, video clips, oral commentary, text screens, and sound effects. He had used a camera, a scanner, video connection, and a tape recorder. Being impressed with the depth of the 12-year-old's understanding of both the subject matter and of the technology, Healy wondered if he had been working with computers since infancy, so she asked him when he started working with computers. He replied: "Two years ago, when I was in fifth grade, I didn't even know anything about computers, and I never even used one until last year. It's not really that hard. You just fuss around until you get it" (*Failure to Connect*, p. 149).

Consider all three important questions about multimedia reports in light of the 12-year-old's King Tut report:

1) *When should students start?* The challenges of producing a multimedia report were certainly met by this 12-year-old even though he admitted to having no knowledge of computers when he was in fifth grade. Perhaps his example implies it's never too late to start.

2) *How should this technology be introduced?* The King Tut example doesn't tell us whether the 12-year-old received direct instruction in how to develop his multimedia report or whether he learned through demonstration, coaching, or independent exploration. What seemed most important was that he was motivated and interested in his topic. Additionally, someone had shown him how to use technology and had modeled many possibilities that he might choose from (slide shows, video clips, scanning and tape recording, etc.). It is apparent from his presentation that he had met the content benchmarks and was an expert on King Tut.

3) *Does the multimedia assignment help the student think more deeply, organize information more effectively, or elaborate a topic more thoroughly?* Based on Healy's assertion that she was impressed with the depth of the 12-year-old's understanding of the subject matter, I would judge the King Tut project to be evidence that the student was helped in all of the above areas.

When evaluating multimedia reports, remember to consider the following questions:

- Were the desired learning outcomes of the project defined ahead of time?
- Were the desired learning outcomes accomplished?
- Does the project demonstrate deep thinking?
- Is the information organized effectively?
- Are assigned topics covered thoroughly?

PLAYING GAMES FOR ENTERTAINMENT

Many parents, caregivers, and educators are worried that some children already spend too much time mesmerized by computer games. Will children become addicted to these games? Will these games corrupt their brains? With the already overcrowded curriculum, it's hard to imagine slots in the school day for video games. What are the cognitive effects of video games for the development of intelligence, creativity, IQ, motivation, attention, problem solving, self-control, and socialization? We don't yet have all the answers to how thinking in a screen-based environment affects the brain. There does seem to be potential for learning to occur from playing video games just as it can occur from watching television or listening to the radio—two other primary sources of entertainment. Let's remain cautiously open-minded as we further consider this new vehicle for learning.

Parents often ask teachers how to balance time spent at home on computers, homework, and TV. In their book, *The Irreducible Needs of Children: What Every Child Must Have to Grow, Learn, and Flourish*, leading pediatrician T. Berry Brazelton and renowned child psychiatrist Stanley Greenspan suggest limiting computer time to about one hour for fourth, fifth, and sixth graders. (Add a little extra time if children are using computers for educational purposes.)

WILL COMPUTERS "DUMB DOWN" YOUR STUDENTS?

Will computers take away opportunities for thinking and cause less learning to happen? Clifford Stoll, author of *Silicon Snake Oil: Second Thoughts on the Information Highway* (1995) presents a daunting prospect: "Computers in classrooms are the filmstrips of the 1990s!" In an interview with *The New York Times*, Stoll recalled his own school days in the 1960s when the teacher stopped teaching and popped in a filmstrip. "We loved them because we didn't have to think for an hour, teachers loved them because they didn't have to teach, and parents loved them because it showed their schools were high-tech. But no learning happened." (Todd Oppenheimer, "The Computer Delusion," *The Atlantic Monthly*, July 1997).

Digital learning may prove to be a boon to children's mental development, but this form of learning must be sufficiently supervised. Teachers must have technology training. They must scaffold computer learning, interact with students one-on-one, and recognize ways to use computers to develop individuals as readers, writers, speakers, and thinkers. One goal for the 21st century must be to find out more about how computers affect the brain. While the technology literacy challenge is important, we must remain committed to children—not computers.

TECHNOLOGY LITERACY BENCHMARKS FOR GRADES FOUR, FIVE, AND SIX

Your students should meet grade-level end-of-year technology benchmarks. The National Educational Technology Standards (NETS) Project, an ongoing initiative of the International Society for Technology in Education (ISTE) provided the initial framework for creating national technology standards in 1998. Based on the NETS framework, the North Carolina State Board of Education published a usable, grade-level specific set of benchmarks for technology (*K-12 Computer/Technology*, 1998). In developing the technology benchmarks for this book, I have drawn largely from the North Carolina standards, finding it to be one of the best sets based on the criteria of specificity, usability, and common sense. I have made adaptations, extensions, and deletions to extend the appeal of these technology standards to a broader audience. The West Virginia standards (*West Virginia Instructional Goals and Objectives*, 2000) also contributed to this set.

I do not pretend to be an expert on technology. In researching this topic, I was surprised to find little conventional wisdom, ecological validity, and research governing technology standards. Perhaps a good set of common sense benchmarks is the best place to start.

FOURTH-GRADE BENCHMARK CHECKLIST FOR TECHNOLOGY LITERACY

NAME: _____

AGE: _____

TEACHER:_____

Record the date in the appropriate box for each question. Comment or give examples in the spaces provided.

BASIC OPERATIONS AND CONCEPTS

KEYBOARD	Not Yet	Some/Sometimes	All/Always
4-1. Practices proper keyboarding techniques for all keys on a keyboard. Uses keyboarding for basic word processing functions such as adjusting uppercase and lowercase lettering, punctuation, and basic adjustments to text such as boldface, italics, and underlining.			

WORD PROCESSING	Not Yet	Some/Sometimes	All/Always
4-2. Edits a word-processing file to make indicated corrections.*			
4-3. Uses the spell-check function to correct the spelling in a word-processing file.			
4-4. Creates, formats, saves, and prints a word-processed document.*			

DATABASE	Not Yet	Some/Sometimes	All/Always
4-5. Defines the parts of a database.*			
4-6. Develops a simple database and enters and edits information as a class activity.*			
4-7. Searches and sorts prepared databases for information to use in classroom projects.*			

SPREADSHEET	Not Yet	Some/Sometimes	All/Always
4-8. Defines basic spreadsheet terms such as cells, rows, columns, workbooks.			

SPREADSHEET	Not Yet	Some/Sometimes	All/Always
4-9. Enters data into a prepared spreadsheet to perform calculations (+, -, x, ÷) and recognizes the changes that occur.*			

TELECOMMUNICATIONS	Not Yet	Some/Sometimes	All/Always
4-10. Uses E-mail as a means of communication.*			
4-11. Visits a web site and uses the mouse to find information.			
4-12. Under supervision, uses search strategies to locate information on the Internet.			

MULTIMEDIA/PRESENTATION	Not Yet	Some/Sometimes	All/Always
4-13. Creates a simple multimedia project and cites sources of copyrighted material.			

ETHICAL BEHAVIOR	Not Yet	Some/Sometimes	All/Always
4-14. Demonstrates the understanding that the violation of copyright law is a crime.			

*   North Carolina Benchmark

FIFTH-GRADE BENCHMARK CHECKLIST FOR TECHNOLOGY LITERACY

NAME: _____

AGE: _____

TEACHER: _____

Record the date in the appropriate box for each question. Comment or give examples in the spaces provided.

BASIC OPERATIONS AND CONCEPTS

KEYBOARD	Not Yet	Some/Sometimes	All/Always
Basic keyboard benchmarks met by end of grade 4.			

WORD PROCESSING	Not Yet	Some/Sometimes	All/Always
Basic word-processing benchmarks met by end of grade 4.			
5.1 Uses basic word processing; formatting of documents becomes routine. (WV)			

DATABASE	Not Yet	Some/Sometimes	All/Always
5-2. Creates/modifies an electronic database.*			
5-3. Searches and sorts information using one criterion.*			
5-4. Adds and deletes record in a database.*			
5-5. Creates a product using information located in a database.*			

SPREADSHEET/GRAPHICS SOFTWARE	Not Yet	Some/Sometimes	All/Always
5-6. Creates/modifies and uses spreadsheets to perform calculations (+, -, x, ÷).*			
5-7. Selects the most appropriate graph to display data and states reason.*			
5-8. Uses graphics software to create graphs and charts. (WV)			

TELECOMMUNICATIONS	Not Yet	Some/Sometimes	All/Always
5-9. Recognizes video conferencing as a method of interactive communication.*			
5-10. Participates in a curriculum-based tele-communications project as a class activity.			

MULTIMEDIA/PRESENTATION	Not Yet	Some/Sometimes	All/Always
5-11. Creates and modifies a multimedia presentation and cites sources of copyrighted materials.			

ETHICAL BEHAVIOR	Not Yet	Some/Sometimes	All/Always
5-12. Demonstrates the understanding that the violation of copyright law is a crime (fourth- grade level benchmark).			

* North Carolina Benchmark
(WV) West Virginia Benchmark

SIXTH-GRADE BENCHMARK CHECKLIST FOR TECNOLOGY LITERACY

NAME: _____

AGE: _____

TEACHER: _____

Record the date in the appropriate box for each question. Comment or give examples in the spaces provided.

BASIC OPERATIONS AND CONCEPTS

KEYBOARD	Not Yet	Some/Sometimes	All/Always
Basic keyboard utilization benchmarks met by end of grade 4.			

WORD PROCESSING	Not Yet	Some/Sometimes	All/Always
Basic word-processing benchmarks met by end of grade 4.			
Uses basic word processing; formatting of documents becomes routine in grade 5.			
6-1. Uses word processing/desktop publishing applications to create documents related to content areas.*			

DATABASE	Not Yet	Some/Sometimes	All/Always
6-2. Chooses to create/modify a database relevant to classroom assignments.			
6-3. Searches and sorts information using more than one database.*			

SPREADSHEET	Not Yet	Some/Sometimes	All/Always
6-4. Creates/modifies and uses spreadsheets to solve real-world problems.*			

TELECOMMUNICATIONS	Not Yet	Some/Sometimes	All/Always
6-5. Applies search strategies to locate and retrieve information via telecommunications.*			

TELECOMMUNICATIONS	Not Yet	Some/Sometimes	All/Always
6-6. Uses telecommunications to share and publish information.*			

MULTIMEDIA/PRESENTATION	Not Yet	Some/Sometimes	All/Always
6-7. Creates multimedia projects related to content areas.			

ETHICAL BEHAVIOR	Not Yet	Some/Sometimes	All/Always
6-8. Models ethical behavior relating to security, privacy, passwords, and personal information.			

* North Carolina Benchmark

POETRY AND LITERACY

Consider poetry in fourth-, fifth-, and sixth-grade classrooms, beginning with Edward Hirsch's inspiring definition.

> **lyric**—The short poem has been practiced for at least 4,500 years. It is one of the necessary forms of human representation, human speech, one of the ways we invent and know ourselves. It is as ancient as recorded literature. It precedes prose in all languages, all civilizations, and it will last as long as human beings take pleasure in playing with words, in combining the sounds of words in unexpected and illuminating ways, in using words to convey deep feeling and perhaps something even deeper than feeling. The lyric poem immerses us in the original waters of consciousness, in the awareness, the aboriginal nature, of being itself. (Hirsch, *How to Read a Poem*, 1999, p. 288)

Those who teach know that we must bring poetry into our classrooms. If it has been done for 4,500 years, is one of the necessary forms of human representation, and helps students invent and know themselves, it must be a literacy benchmark. I have found no research-based study and little conventional wisdom to guide poetry benchmarks. I thought it appropriate, therefore, to close the discussion of the literacy map with a call to further children's love for poetry.

Poetry seems to be banished from many classrooms. This is disturbing in light of the fact that poetry is a part of humanness itself. Each student enters your classroom with poetry inside him or herself. A deeper awareness and capacity to experience poetry, like the capacity to read, write, or spell, is a crucial literacy goal.

Poems should be felt, experienced, savored, memorized, read in solitude, and heard aloud. Often the way poetry is taught makes students feel uncomfortable. I suspect too many of us remember sober analyses that left our heads spinning with definitions of "dactyl" and memorized phrases, such as "a five-stress decasyllabic line," to match with "iambic pentameter." It's easier to know what a poem is than to define it or unpack it and fold it up just like the teacher wants it to be folded. Hirsch says, "We cannot know poetry by any intrinsic properties of poetry itself, but by our contact with it. It has an intensity which cannot be denied" (1999, p. 300). Following his lead, I suppose the benchmark for fourth, fifth, and sixth grade should assure contact with poetry and a hope for some intense response. You should just lay it out and let the child fold it up if he or she can use it. The teaching goal should be to bring poetry into your classroom and make opportunities for these verbal transactions between a writer and a reader or a listener.

What's supposed to happen when you bring poetry into your classroom? Emily Dickinson's definition of poetry provides great illumination:

> If I read a book [and] it makes my whole body so cold no fire can ever warm me I know *that* is poetry. If I feel physically as if the top of my head were taken off, I know *that* is poetry. These are the only way I know it. Is there any other way?
> (*The Letters of Emily Dickinson*, Thomas H. Johnson, ed.)

How many poems can you recite from memory? How many have you recited this year in your classroom? We seem to be losing the oral tradition of poetry. A few years ago I went to see *Sophie's Choice*. I was stirred by an Emily Dickinson poem the narrator recites at the end of the movie. My personal awakening to the power of poetry and my discovery of a wonderful oral tradition of poetry in elementary classrooms coincided.

> Ample make this Bed—
> Make this Bed with Awe—
> In it wait till Judgment break
> Excellent and Fair.
>
> Be its Mattress straight—
> Be its Pillow round—
> Let no Sunrise' yellow noise
> Interrupt this Ground—

I remember sitting immobile as this poem saturated my body—a surging, swelling, stirring, and sweeping of something inside me came spilling out my tear ducts. It was the moment poetry breathed new life in me. After that experience, I started reading *The Complete Poems of Emily Dickinson* containing all of her 1,775 poems. On my frequent two and one-half hour commutes from my home in North Carolina to Atlanta, I would memorize my favorites and eventually had quite a repertoire. Many of the poems are still with me. They have changed the way I think, the way I write, and the way I listen.

Once poetry inhabited me I started finding it everywhere, including selections of fiction and nonfiction. I read *Out of Africa* by Isak Dinesen and found sections that I just had to memorize. Her words painted portraits of the African landscape that "physically blew the top of my head off," to borrow words from Emily Dickinson, and I still feel like I have been to Africa.

> If I know a song of Africa—I thought,
> Of the giraffe,
> And the new African moon lying on her back.

Of the ploughs in the fields, and the sweaty faces of the coffee-
      pickers,
      Does Africa know a song of me?
      Would the air over the plain quiver with a colour that I
      had had on,
      Or the children invent a game in which my name was,
Or the full moon throw a shadow over the gravel of the drive
      that was like me,
      Or would the eagles of Ngong look out for me?
(Dinesen, Isak. 1937. *Out of Africa.* New York: Random House, Inc.)

During this personal rebirth of a love for poetry, I was teaching Jamaican teachers in my university's overseas extension program, traveling to Jamaica for stints of up to one month. There I witnessed the oral tradition of poetry thriving in elementary school classrooms. I visited schools all over the island. Sometimes I found overcrowded classrooms, with as many as 40 children cramped in close quarters on wooden benches. Supplies and books were scarce. What impressed me, though, was a wonderful oral tradition for poetry. In each classroom children had a repertoire of poems they loved to recite—in English and in patois, the native vernacular. The poems were experienced with feeling and emotion, often with drama—a spectacular example of children taking pleasure in playing with words.

Why don't we do this in American schools? I remember my father and grandmother talking about my great grandfather's one-room American schoolhouse. I imagined it must have resembled what I saw in Jamaica. In the past, Americans enjoyed a wonderful oral tradition of poetry. Why have we lost this poetic oral tradition?

Children can make poetry with a mouthful of words and opportunities to reflect upon their unique human experience. You probably have experienced the poetic moment when wisdom spews out of the mouth or out of a pen of a child. It made you laugh or filled you with emotion.

Your students are already "into" poetry in rap songs, country music, songs or prayers learned in houses of worship, songs or riddles or jokes from pop culture. Poetry is inside each one of them. Shouldn't we expand upon this interest?

Think of teaching poetry as giving children opportunities to take pleasure in playing with words. Start out light, choosing fun poems that will make them fall out of their seats laughing. Throw in a serious one on a serious occasion. Bring in poems that you love and let children learn about poetry from the poem. Don't test children on poetry. Inspire them with a poem.

I believe the fourth-, fifth-, and sixth-grade literacy map should include a rebirth of exposure and opportunity to experience poetry. It's a natural 4,500 year-old tradition that needs to be exploited. With that in mind, I end *The Literacy Map* with five benchmarks for poetry. Each child should:

- Have a repertoire of five favorite poems he or she can recite from memory.
- Share poetry with an audience sometime during the year.
- Find one new poem he or she loves and memorize it this year in your classroom.
- Write an original poem and share it sometime during the year.
- Keep a poetry journal of favorite poems.

Ask children to give you poems as a gift at the end of the year. Then give one back to them.

SAMPLE SCHEDULES
(From Lynn Pott's Classroom)

There is no perfect elementary school schedule that meets all scheduling contingincies. The authentic schedules listed below—though imperfect— reflect the range and flexibility needed in creating schedules that work.

SCHEDULE 1 (Grades 4–6)

8:35-9:15	Physical Education / Music
9:20-11:30	Literacy Block (Reading Workshop/Writing Workshop)
11:35-12:05	Recess / Lunch
12:20-12:50	Science
12:50-1:35	Math
1:35-2:00	Spelling Vocabulary / Art (Thursdays 1:35-2:25)
2:00-2:45	Social Studies

Note: Literacy Block is uninterrupted—no pullouts.

SCHEDULE 2 (Grades 4–6)

8:35-9:00	Opening
9:00-9:55	Physical Education / Music
10:00-10:45	Social Studies / Science
10:45-11:40	Math
11:40-12:25	Writing Workshop
12:30-1:05	Lunch / Recess
1:05-2:15	Self-selected Reading / Art (Tuesdays 1:40-2:30)
2:15-3:00	Guided Reading
3:00-3:15	Spelling Workshop
3:15-3:30	Read Aloud

Note: Physical Education is 25 minutes; Vocal Music is 30 minutes.

SCHEDULE 3 (Grades 4–6)

8:45-9:00	Opening
9:00-9:55	Math
9:55-10:45	Physical Education / Music
10:45-11:30	Social Studies / Science
11:30-11:45	Spelling
11:45-12:45	Lunch / Recess
12:45-2:15	Literacy Block / Art (Tuesdays 1:40-2:30)
2:15-3:30	Literacy Block

Note: Physical Education is 20 minutes; Vocal Music is 30 minutes.

FOURTH-GRADE VOCABULARY ACTIVITIES

Shiloh by Phyllis Reynolds Naylor contains some vocabulary indigenous to its rural West Virginia setting. The words and phrases are not difficult for most fourth graders, but there are expressions that might be unfamiliar to some students.

TEACHING ACTIVITY: CONTEXTUAL ANALYSIS

slinking (p. 13) ". . . about fifteen yards off, there's this shorthaired dog not making any kind of noise, just slinking along with his head down, watching me, tail between his legs like he's hardly got the right to breathe."

Teaching Hint: Students get a mental image of the dog sneaking along, low to the ground, feeling either fear or guilt. The clues to the dog's movement are head down, tail between legs, noiseless, and not feeling worthy to even breathe. Students may also picture a thief or prowler moving in this manner.

lean-to (p. 44) "I take the planks up to Shiloh's pen and make him a lean-to at one end, to protect him from rain."

Teaching Hint: From the sentences around the word *lean-to*, we know it is something a young boy can easily make out of wooden planks. It has one open side and is used for protection from the rain. The word *lean* also gives a hint about the slant of the roof.

TEACHING ACTIVITY: ACTING OUT WORDS

In *Shiloh* there are words that describe dog actions. Act out or use the following words in a role-playing situation. Then discuss which words might also be associated with human behavior: grovel (p. 13), cringe (p. 14), whimper (p.14), barreling (p. 15), yelps (p. 15), gulps (p. 46), nuzzling (p. 47), panting (p. 47), snarl (p. 87), wince (p. 89).

Demonstrate emotions using the following words from the story: concern (p. 21), flustered (p. 23), tense (p. 44), restless (p. 49), greedy (p. 56), suspicious (p. 63), envy (p. 66), mournful (p. 108), jubilation (p. 132), disgusted (p. 133).

TEACHING ACTIVITY: ROOT WORD OR AFFIX ANALYSIS

Discuss which suffix would be added to the following root words to mean "full of." Display these words from *Shiloh* on chart paper and add to the chart as students find other examples.

full of greed (p. 56)	greedy
full of suspicion (p. 63)	suspicious
full of envy (p. 66)	envious
full of enthusiasm (p. 99)	enthusiastic
full of spite (p. 128)	spiteful
full of jubilation (p. 132)	jubilant
full of pity (p. 132)	pitiful

TEACHING ACTIVITY: VISUAL REPRESENTATION

Students visually represent the following words found in *Shiloh* by drawing a picture, finding photographs, or creating a drawing from the letters in the word to represent the meaning of the word.

propeller (p. 16)	jowls (p. 50)
coop (p. 20)	route (p. 52)
buck (p. 32)	trousers (p. 90)
sickle (p. 34)	stethoscope (p. 91)
lean-to (p. 44)	scenery (p. 118)
saucer (p. 49)	grin (p. 129)

SIXTH-GRADE VOCABULARY ACTIVITIES

Roll of Thunder, Hear My Cry by Mildred D. Taylor contains a lot of rich vocabulary. In the first chapter, there are over 200 words that might be unfamiliar to students. This underscores the dilemma of choosing the best words to study. Keep in mind that your goal is to develop vocabulary building consciousness and to equip your students with strategies they can use to build their own vocabularies. Think of word study as a habit that students develop rather than a list of words students memorize. Consciously match the words you select to the individuals in your classroom based on their interests and needs. Below are sample activities.

TEACHING ACTIVITY: CONTEXTUAL ANALYSIS

mar (p. 3) "Always meticulously neat, six year old Little Man never allowed dirt or tears or stain to mar anything he owned."

Teaching Hint: Since dirt and tears and stain keep things from being neat and in good condition, the word *mar* obviously means to ruin, damage, or destroy. *Is there anything in our classroom that has been marred? How or why?*

spewing (p. 13) "Little Man turned round and watched saucer-eyed as a bus bore down on him spewing clouds of red dust like a huge, yellow dragon breathing fire."

Teaching Hint: The comparison of the bus spewing red dust to a dragon breathing fire gives a clue to the word's meaning. (Have students make a mental picture.) Realizing that *spew* means to gush out, spurt, or emit should give them ideas about other things that can be spewed—a volcano spews lava, words (usually negative) spew from someone's mouth, water spews from a whale's blow hole.

gleaned (p. 16) "...after today a number of the older students would not be seen again for a month or two, not until the last puff of cotton had been gleaned from the fields..."

Teaching Hint: It could be inferred from the content that *gleaned* is an action done to the cotton, and the students can't return to school until it is done. Most will realize that cotton is picked, and that the word must refer to gathering, collecting, picking up, or extracting.

TEACHING ACTIVITY: ACTING OUT WORDS

Each of these words describe different ways people speak or communicate. By acting them out, students will learn the differences among them: murmured, stammered, whispered, exclaimed, demanded, mumbled. Be sure to discuss the differences in volume, (softest sounds would be *whispered*, *murmured*, and *mumbled*—while loudest would be *demanded* and *exclaimed*); compare when you would speak in an animated or subdued manner; and compare the way each word was used in the novel.

Act out the following words which have to do with body movement: nudged, reversed, interfere, quivered, rearranged, propped (elbows on knees), trudged, unveiling, depositing, applauded, grasping, restrain.

TEACHING ACTIVITY: BASE WORD AND ROOT WORD OR AFFIX ANALYSIS

Many words are derived from Greek and Latin root words. We make additions to base words to make new words. The additions (affixes) may be prefixes or suffixes.

Compare the Latin roots *vis-* and *aud-*. Make a chart with the words *visible* and *audible* from the novel. Brainstorm other words with these roots to reinforce the meanings: vision, television, visual, visibility, invisible, envision, visit, visualize, visor, visionary, visage, vista; auditory, audio, audition, audience, auditorium, audiometer, inaudible.

Discuss the meaning of the prefix *semi-* (half or partly) as in the word *semi-circle* found in *Roll of Thunder, Hear My Cry*. Brainstorm other words and record on a chart: semi-annual, semiconscious, semifinals, semi-truck, semicolon, semiprecious.

TEACHING ACTIVITY: VISUAL REPRESENTATION

The following words from Chapter 1 in *Roll of Thunder, Hear My Cry* would be easy to draw or sketch once students have discussed them. It might be necessary to show pictures of some of the words first: cuffs, imprisoned, potbellied stove, belfry, tiered, sloping.

Ask students to bring in pictures or examples of the following:

scarlet (scarlet-colored objects, such as a scarf, fall maple leaf, etc.).
plantation (photograph or drawing from a history book)
corduroy
tarpaulin
threadbare (old jeans with tattered knees or old shirt with frayed elbows)

TEACHING ACTIVITY: VOCABULARY FRIENDLY FEUD GAME

This game gives students practice using targeted vocabulary words from a novel. The object of the game is to guess the meaning of the targeted words. Several target words are put on an overhead projector or chalkboard. Divide the class into teams of three or four. Decide who starts first. The teacher then gives a clue word, or synonym, for a target word from the displayed list. The first student must guess the mystery word that matches the synonym. No consultation with teammates is allowed at this point. If the student guesses the mystery word from the first clue, the team is awarded ten points. If an incorrect guess is given, the next team member is given a clue. If the mystery word is guessed correctly from the second clue, the team gets eight points. As the game continues, each clue is worth fewer points for the team. If four clues are given and the word is not correctly guessed, the other team can "steal" the answer and receive ten points. (The "stealing" team can consult with teammates when deciding on the correct answer.) The clue words are given from most difficult to least difficult corresponding to the greater number of points awarded. When the target word has been correctly identified, the other team is given a new word. If the word is "stolen," the "stealing" team gets the next word. Continue play until a certain number of words are identified, a particular point value is reached, or a time limit is met.

Words for Vocabulary Friendly Feud

Target words

raucous	remainder	emaciated	suspicious	morosely

Clue words

boisterous	excess	malnourished	wary	downcast
rowdy	surplus	famished	cautious	miserable
shrill	leftover	starved	watchful	sorrowful
noisy	extra	skinny	careful	sad

Target words

disdainfully	sparsely	consisting	eventually	adjust

Clue words

contemptuous	dearth	comprise	imminent	rectify
scornful	scarcity	include	momentary	revamp
resentful	scant	contain	straightaway	modify
bitter	shortage	involve	shortly	rearrange

The Gentry Spelling Grade Level Placement Test

GRADE FIVE

1. neighbor
2. parties
3. rotten
4. worst
5. laid
6. manners
7. parents
8. hungry
9. subject
10. claim
11. unknown
12. American
13. officer
14. prove
15. library
16. yawn
17. midnight
18. steady
19. prepare
20. village

GRADE SIX

1. jewel
2. thief
3. avenue
4. arrangement
5. theme
6. system
7. written
8. depot
9. ruin
10. yield
11. seize
12. difference
13. interview
14. zero
15. hymn
16. lettuce
17. burden
18. canvas
19. grocery
20. lawyer

GRADE SEVEN

1 possession
2. yacht
3. thorough
4. gymnasium
5. interrupt
6. athletic
7. secretary
8. agriculture
9. scientist
10. anchor
11. announce
12. revenue
13. patient
14. pressure
15. straighten
16. establish
17. laboratory
18. cashier
19. wrath
20. intelligent

GRADE EIGHT

1. fierce
2. analyze
3. committee
4. predominant
5. pursue
6. chemically
7. financial
8. appropriateness
9. cheetah
10. schedule
11. autobiographical
12. executive
13. coincidence
14. seniority
15. restaurant
16. alliteration
17. grievance
18. vengeance
19. guarantee
20 columnist

From *My Kid Can't Spell* by J. Richard Gentry. Published by Heinemann.

BOOK LIST GRADES 3–6
(LEVELS O-Z)

LEVEL O
Grade Three

Title	Author	Publisher
Adventures of Ali Baba Bernstein	Hurwitz, Johanna	Avon Books
Beezus and Ramona	Cleary, Beverly	Avon Books
Boxcar Children: Bicycle Mystery	Warner, Gertrude Chandler	Albert Whitman
Bunnicula	Howe, James	Avon Books
Make a Wish, Molly	Cohen, Barbara	Bantam Doubleday Dell
Mario's Mayan Journey	McCunney, Michelle	Mondo Publishing
Matilda	Dahl, Roald	Puffin Books
Miss Geneva's Lantern	Lake, Mary Dixon	Mondo Publishing
The Whipping Boy	Fleischman, Sid	Troll

LEVEL P
Grade Three

Title	Author	Publisher
Amelia Earhart	Parlin, John	Bantam Doubleday Dell
Baseball's Best, Five True Stories	Gutelle, Andrew	Random House
Baseball's Greatest Pitchers	Kramer, S. A.	Random House
Five Brave Explorers	Hudson, Wade	Scholastic
George's Marvelous Medicine	Dahl, Roald	Puffin Books
Helen Keller	Graff, Stewart and Polly Anne Graff	Bantam Doubleday Dell
Jesse Owens: Olympic Hero	Sabin, Francene	Troll
One Day in the Tropical Rain Forest	George, Jean Craighead	HarperTrophy
A Pony Named Shawney	Small, Mary	Mondo Publishing
Sugar Cakes Cyril	Gershator, Phillis	Mondo Publishing

LEVEL Q
Grade Four

Title	Author	Publisher
Anastasia Krupnik	Lowry, Lois	Bantam Doubleday Dell
Charlotte's Web	White, E.B.	HarperTrophy
Homer Price	McCloskey, Robert	Scholastic
James and the Giant Peach	Dahl, Roald	The Penguin Group
Little House on the Prairie	Wilder, Laura Ingalls	HarperTrophy
A Pocketful of Goobers: Story of George Washington Carver	Mitchell, Barbara	Carolrhoda Books
Princesses Don't Wear Jeans	Bellingham, Brenda	Mondo Publishing
Tales of a Fourth Grade Nothing	Blume, Judy	Bantam Doubleday Dell
There's A Boy in the Girls' Bathroom	Sachar, Louis	Alfred A. Knopf, Inc.
The Velveteen Rabbit	Williams, Margery	Hearst Corp.

LEVEL R
Grade Four

Title	Author	Publisher
And Then What Happened to Paul Revere?	Fritz, Jean	Scholastic
Caddie Woodlawn	Ryrie Brink, Carol	Bantam Doubleday Dell
Charlie and the Chocolate Factory	Dahl, Roald	Bantam Doubleday Dell
Deadbolts and Dinkles	Tapp, Kathy Kennedy	Mondo Publishing
Flying Solo	Fletcher, Ralph	Houghton Mifflin
Forest Fires: Run for Your Life!	Nobisso, Josephine	Mondo Publishing
Misty of Chincoteague	Henry, Marguerite	Scholastic
Sarah, Plain and Tall	MacLachlan, Patricia	HarperTrophy
Shiloh	Naylor, Phyllis Reynolds	Bantam Doubleday Dell
Stuart Little	White, E.B.	HarperTrophy

LEVEL S
Grades Four/Five

Title	Author	Publisher
Crocodilians	Short, J. and B. Bird	Mondo Publishing
The Cry of the Crow	George, Jean Craighead	HarperTrophy
Fifth Grade: Here Comes Trouble	McKenna, Colleen O'Shaughnessy	Scholastic
From the Mixed-up Files of Mrs. Basil E. Frankweiler	Konigsburg, E.L.	Bantam Doubleday Dell
Insects	Bird, Bettina	Mondo Publishing
Jacob Have I Loved	Paterson, Katherine	HarperTrophy
My Teacher Fried My Brains	Coville, Bruce	Pocket Books
Poppy	Avi	Avon Books
Story of Muhammad Ali: The Heavyweight Champion of the World	Denenberg, Barry	Dell Publishing
The Trumpet of the Swan	White, E.B.	HarperTrophy
Where Do You Think You're Going, Christopher Columbus?	Fritz, Jean	Putnam & Grosset

LEVEL T
Grades Four/Five

Title	Author	Publisher
Baby	MacLachlan, Patricia	Language for Learning Assoc.
A Ballad of the Civil War	Stolz, Mary	HarperTrophy
Blubber	Blume, Judy	Language for Learning Assoc.
But I'll Be Back Again	Rylant, Cynthia	William Morrow
Gorillas	Burgel, P. and M. Hartwig	Carolrhoda Books
Harry Potter and the Prisoner of Azkaban	Rowling, J.K.	Scholastic
Harry Potter and the Sorcerer's Stone	Rowling, J.K.	Scholastic
My Hiroshima	Morimoto, Junko	The Penguin Group
Sing Down the Moon	O'Dell, Scott	Language for Learning Assoc.
Tracker	Paulsen, Gary	Harcourt Brace

LEVEL U
Grade Five

Title	Author	Publisher
Benjamin Franklin	Kent, Deborah	Scholastic
Bridge to Terabithia	Paterson, Katherine	HarperTrophy
The Girl in the Window	Yeo, Wilma	Scholastic
Julie of the Wolves	George, Jean Craighead	HarperCollins
My Side of the Mountain	George, Jean Craighead	The Penguin Group
A Place Called Heartbreak: A Story of Vietnam	Myers, Walter Dean	Steck Vaughn
Remember the Ladies: The First Women's Rights Convention	Johnston, Norma	Scholastic
Tuck Everlasting	Babbitt, Natalie	Farrar, Straus & Giroux
Woodsong	Paulsen, Gary	The Penguin Group
Wringer	Spinelli, Jerry	HarperTrophy

LEVEL V
Grades Five/Six

Title	Author	Publisher
The Biggest Klutz in Fifth Grade	Wallace, Bill	Simon & Schuster
Holes	Sachar, Louis	Farrar, Straus & Giroux
Island of the Blue Dolphins	O'Dell, Scott	Bantam Doubleday Dell
The Riddle of the Rosetta Stone	Giblin, James Cross	HarperTrophy
The Underground Railroad	Bial, Raymond	Houghton Mifflin
A Wrinkle in Time	L'Engle, Madeline	Bantam Doubleday Dell

LEVEL W
Grades Five/Six

Title	Author	Publisher
A Blue-Eyed Daisy	Rylant, Cynthia	Simon & Schuster
Great Whales: The Gentle Giants	Lauber, Patricia	Henry Holt & Co.
Maniac Magee	Spinelli, Jerry	Scholastic/ HarperTrophy
Maya Angelou: Greeting the Morning	King, Sarah E.	The Millbrook Press
Moccasin Trail	McGraw, Eloise	Scholastic
Phoenix Rising	Hesse, Karen	The Penguin Group
Roll of Thunder, Hear My Cry	Taylor, Mildred D.	The Penguin Group
Who Is Carrie?	Collier, James Lincoln and C. Collier	Bantam Doubleday Dell
The Witch of Blackbird Pond	Speare, Elizabeth George	Bantam Doubleday Dell
You Want Women to Vote, Lizzie Stanton?	Fritz, Jean	The Penguin Group

LEVEL X
Grade Six

Title	Author	Publisher
The Dark Is Rising	Cooper, Susan	Macmillan
Let the Circle Be Unbroken	Taylor, Mildred D.	The Penguin Group
M.C. Higgins the Great	Hamilton, Virginia	Macmillan
Novio Boy	Soto, Gary	Harcourt Brace
The Road to Memphis	Taylor, Mildred D.	The Penguin Group
Sarah Bishop	O'Dell, Scott	Scholastic
Where the Red Fern Grows	Rawls, Wilson	Bantam Doubleday Dell
The Yearling	Rawlings, Marjorie Kinnan	Simon & Schuster

LEVEL Y
Grade Six

Title	Author	Publisher
Call of the Wild	London, Jack	Signet Classics
The Diary of Anne Frank	Frank, Anne	Bantam Books
The Giver	Lowry, Lois	Bantam Doubleday Dell
Jackaroo	Voigt, Cynthia	Scholastic
Jesse	Soto, Gary	Scholastic
Living Up the Street	Soto, Gary	Bantam Doubleday Dell
The Pushcart War	Merrill, Jean	Bantam Doubleday Dell
Where the Lilies Bloom	Cleavers, Vera and Bill Cleavers	HarperTrophy

LEVEL Z
Grade Six

Title	Author	Publisher
The Adventures of Tom Sawyer	Twain, Mark	Scholastic
The Contender	Lipsythe, Robert	HarperTrophy
Flowers for Algernon	Keyes, Daniel	Harcourt Brace
From the Notebooks of Melanin Sun	Woodson, Jacqueline	Scholastic
The Hobbit	Tolkien, J.R.R.	Ballantine Books
The Outsiders	Hinton, S.E.	The Penguin Group
Summer of My German Soldier	Green, Bette	Penguin Putnam Books for Young Readers
Treasure Island	Stevenson, Robert Louis	Scholastic
Woman Hollering Creek	Cisneros, Sandra	Random House

* Level references adapted from *Guiding Readers and Writers Grades 3–6* by Irene C. Fountas and Gay Su Pinnell.

REFERENCES

Adams, Marilyn. 1990. *Beginning to Read: Thinking and Learning About Print.* Cambridge, MA: MIT Press.

Allington, Richard L. 2001. *What Really Matters for Struggling Readers: Designing Research-Based Programs.* New York: Addison Wesley Educational Publishers, Inc.

———— 2001. *What Really Matters for Struggling Readers.* New York: Addison Wesley Longman.

————2000. "What Really Matters for Struggling Readers" Keynote. Western Reading Recovery & Early Literacy Conference. Portland, OR. October 28, 2000.

————1984. "Content Coverage and Contextual Reading in Reading Groups." *Journal of Reading Behavior*, 16, 85-96.

———— 1983. "The Reading Instruction Provided Readers of Differing Abilities." *Elementary School Journal*, 83, 548-559.

———— 1980. "Teacher Interruption Behaviors During Primary Grade Oral Reading." *Journal of Educational Psychology*, 72, 371-377.

———— 1977. "If They Don't Read Much, How They Ever Gonna Get Good?" *Journal of Reading*, 21, 57-61.

Anderson, Richard C. and P. Wilson, L. Fielding. 1998. "Growth in Reading and How Children Spend Their Time Outside of School." *Reading Research Quarterly*, 23(3), 285-303.

Anderson, Richard. C. and E. H. Hiebert, J. A. Scott, I. A. G. Wilkinson. 1985. *Becoming a Nation of Readers: The Report of the Commission on Reading.* Washington, DC: The National Institute of Education.

Atwell, Nancie. 1987. *In the Middle: Writing, Reading, and Learning with Adolescents.* Portsmouth, NH: Heinemann.

Bear, Donald R., and Marcia Invernizzi, Shane Templeton, Francine Johnston. 2000. *Words Their Way: Word Study for Phonics, Vocabulary, and Spelling Instruction.* (2nd Edition). Englewood Cliffs, NJ: Prentice Hall.

Beers, J. W. and E. Henderson. 1997. "A Study of Orthographic Concepts Among First Graders." *Research in the Teaching of English,* 11, 133-148.

Betts, Emmett A. 1946. *Foundations of Reading Instruction.* New York: American.

Bjorklund, David F. 1995. *Children's Thinking: Developmental Function and Individual Differences.* New York: Brooks/Cole Publishing Company.

Bloom, Harold. 2000. *How to Read and Why.* New York: Scribner.

Brazelton, T. Berry and Stanley I. Greenspan. 2000. *The Irreducible Needs of Children: What Every Child Must Have to Grow, Learn, and Flourish.* Cambridge, MA: Perseus Publishing.

Bryant, N, D. 1975. *Diagnostic Test of Basic Decoding Skills.* New York: Columbia University, Teachers College.

Burmeister, L. 1975. *Words—From Print To Meaning.* Reading, MA: Addison-Wesley.

Caulkins, Lucy. 1983. *Lessons From a Child.* Portsmouth, NH: Heinemann.

Chambers, Aidan. 1996. *Tell Me: Children, Reading, and Talk.* Portland, ME: Stenhouse.

Chomsky, Carol. 1970. "Reading, Writing, and Phonology." *Harvard Educational Review,* 40, 287-309.

Computer/Technology Skills Curriculum. 1998. State Board of Education/ Department of Public Instruction. *http://www.dpi.state.nc.us/curriculum/ computer.skills/*

Cunningham, Patricia M. 1995. *Phonics They Use: Words for Reading and Writing* (2nd Edition). New York: HarperCollins.

Cunningham, Patricia M., Dorothy P. Hall, James W. Cunningham. 2000. *Guided Reading the Four-Blocks™ Way:* Greensboro, NC: Carson-Dellosa Publishing Company, Inc.

Daniels, Harvey. 1994. *Literature Circles: Voice and Choice in the Student-Centered Classroom.* York, ME: Stenhouse.

Daniels, Harvey. 2002. *Literature Circles: Voice and Choice in Book Clubs and Reading Groups* (2nd Edition). York, ME: Stenhouse.

Davis, Kevin. 2000. "The Little Einstein on Campus," *USA Today*. November 27, 2000, p. 13A.

Dyson, A. H. (Ed.). 1989. *Collaboration Through Reading and Writing: Exploring Possibilities*. Urbana, IL: National Council of Teachers of English.

Ehri, Linnea C. 1997. "Learning to Read and Learning to Spell Are One and the Same, Almost." Charles A. Perfetti, Laurence Reiben and Michel Fayol (Eds.), *Learning to Spell: Research, Theory, and Practice Across Languages*. Chapter 13, (pp. 237-269). London: Lawrence Erlbaum Associates.

_____ 1984. "How Orthography Alters Spoken Language Competencies in Children Learning to Read and Spell." J. Downing and R. Valtin (Eds.), *Language Awareness and Learning to Read* (pp. 119-147). New York: Springer-Verlag.

Ehri, Linnea C. and L. Wilce. 1985. "Movement into reading: Is the first stage of printed word learning visual or phonetic?" *Reading Research Quarterly*, 20, 163-179.

Elkonin, D. B. 1993. "The Psychology of Mastery Elements of Reading." B. Simon and J. Simon (Eds.), *Educational Psychology in the USSR* (pp. 165-179). London: Routledge and Kegan Paul.

"The English Language Arts Standards," 1998. New York State Standards Document.

Feldgus, Eileen G. and Isabell Cardonick. 1999. *Kid Writing: A Systematic Approach to Phonics, Journals, and Writing Workshop*. Bothell, WA: The Wright Group.

Fletcher, Ralph. 2000. "Craft Lessons to Improve the Quality of Student Writing." Session, Twenty-eighth Annual Conference of the Maryland International Reading Association, March 15, 2000. Baltimore, MD.

Fletcher, Ralph, and JoAnn Portalupi. 1998. *Craft Lessons: Teaching Writing K-8*. York, ME: Stenhouse Publishers.

Fountas, Irene C. and Gay Su Pinnell. 2001. *Guiding Readers and Writers Grades 3-6*. Portsmouth, NH: Heinemann.

_____ 1996. *Guided Reading*. Portsmouth, NH: Heinemann.

Ganske, Kathy. 2000. *Word Journeys*. New York: Guilford Publication.

Gentry, J. Richard. 2000a. *The Literacy Map: Guiding Children to Where They Need to Be (K-3)*. New York: Mondo.

_____ 2000b. "A Retrospective on Invented Spelling and a Look Forward." *The Reading Teacher*. 54 (3), 318-332.

_____ 2000c. *Spelling Connections*. Columbus, OH: Zaner-Bloser.

_____ 1997. *My Kid Can't Spell*. Portsmouth, NH: Heinemann.

_____ 1997. *A Study of the Orthographic Strategies of Beginning Readers*. Unpublished doctoral dissertation. University of Virginia, Charlottesville.

_____ 1982. "An Analysis of Developmental Spelling in GNYS at WRK." *The Reading Teacher*. 36, 192-200.

_____ 1978. "Early Spelling Strategies." *The Elementary School Journal*, 79, 88-92.

_____1977. "Spelling Strategies." *Instructor*. New York: Scholastic. p. 77

Gentry, J. Richard and Karen R. Harris, Jerry, Zutell, Steve Graham. 1998. *Spell It—Write!* Columbus, OH: Zaner-Bloser.

Gough, P. B. and C.Juel, P. L Griffith. 1992. "Reading, Spelling, and the Orthographic Cipher." P.B. Gough, L.C. Ehri, and R. Treiman (Eds.), *Reading Acquisition* (pp. 35-48). Hillsdale, NJ: Lawrence Erlbaum Associates.

Graves, Donald. 1994. *A Fresh Look at Writing*. Portsmouth, NH: Heinemann.

_____ 1983. *Writing: Teachers and Children at Work*. Portsmouth, NH: Heinemann.

Griffith, P. L. and M. W. Olson. 1992. "Phonemic Awareness Helps Beginning Readers Break the Code." *The Reading Teacher*, 45, 516-523.

Hammond, Dorsey and Taffy E. Raphael. 1999. *Early Literacy Instruction for the New Millennium*. Grand Rapids, MI: Michigan Reading Association/ Center for the Improvement of Early Reading Achievement.

Hansen, J. 1987. *When Writers Read*. Portsmouth, NH: Heinemann.

Hansen, J. and T. Newkirk, D. Graves (Eds.). 1985. *Breaking Ground: Teachers Relate Reading and Writing in the Elementary School*. Portsmouth, NH: Heinemann.

Healy, Jane M. 1998. *Failure to Connect: How Computers Affect Our Children's Minds—and What We Can Do About It*. New York: Simon & Schuster Inc.

Henderson, Edmund. 1981. *Learning to Read and Spell: The Child's Knowledge of Words*. DeKalb, IL: Northern Illinois University Press.

Hill, Peter W. and Carmel A. Crevola. 1999. "Chapter 6: The Role of Standards in Educational Reform for the 21st Century." David Marsh (Ed.) *Association for Supervision and Curriculum Development Yearbook.*

Hirsch, Edward. 1999. *How to Read a Poem.* New York: Harcourt Brace and Company.

Hynes, Myrna. 2000. "'I Read for Facts:' Reading Nonfiction in a Fictional World." *Language Arts,* 77, 6, 485-495.

Keene, Ellin O. and Susan Zimmermann. 1997. *Mosaic of Thought: Teaching Comprehension in a Reader's Workshop.* Portsmouth, NH: Heinemann.

Laminack, Lester and Katie Wood. 1996. *Spelling in Use: Looking Closely at Spelling in Whole Language Classrooms.* Urbana, IL: National Council of Teachers of English (p. 65).

Levin, J. R. and M. E., Levin, L.D. Glasman, M. B. Nordwall. 1992. "Mnemonic Vocabulary Instruction: Additional Effectiveness Evidence." *Contemporary Educational Psychology,* 17(2), 156-174.

Levine, J. and C. Baroudi, M. Levine. 1996. *Internet for Dummies.* Boston: HarperAudio, 1996.

Mann, Dale, and Charol Shakeshaft, Jonathan Becker , Robert Kettkamp. 1999. "West Virginia Story: Achievement Gains from a Statewide Comprehensive Instructional Technology Program 1999: What Impact Does Technology Have on Learning?" Milken Family Foundation Publication in collaboration with the West Virginia Department of Education. *http://www.mff.org/publications/publications.taf?page=155*

Maria, K. 1990. *Reading Comprehension Instruction: Issues and Strategies.* Timonium, MD: York Press.

Marzano, Robert J., and Diane E. Paynter, John S. Kendall, Debra Pickering, Lorraine Marzano. 1991. *Literacy Plus Teacher Reference Book to Words in Semantic Clusters.* Columbus, OH: Zaner-Bloser, Inc.

Masonheimer, P. and P. Drum, L. Ehri. 1984. "Does Environmental Print Identification Lead Children Into Word Reading?" *Journal of Reading Behavior,* 16, 257-272.

McKeown, M. G. and I. L. Beck, R. C. Omanson, M. T. Pople. 1985. "Some Effects of the Nature and Frequency of Vocabulary Instruction on the Knowledge and Use of Words." *Reading Research Quarterly,* 20(5), 522-535.

Mesmer, Heidi Anne E. 1999. "Scaffolding a Crucial Transition Using Text with Some Decodability." *The Reading Teacher.* 53, 2, 130-141.

Moats, Louisa. 2000. Sixth General Session. Keystone State Reading Association Thirty-third Annual Conference. Seven Springs Mountain Resort, PA. October 24, 2000.

Morrison, Toni. 1992. *Playing in the Dark: Whiteness and the Literary Imagination.* Cambridge, MA: Harvard University Press.

Murphy, Sharon and Curt Dudley-Marling. 2000. "Editors' Pages," *Language Arts,* 77 (6), 478.

Murray, Donald. 1982. *Learning by Teaching: Selected Articles on Writing and Teaching.* Portsmouth, NH: Heinemann.

National Education Technology Standards for Students. 1998. The Milken Exchange and the International Society for Technology in Education (ISTE) *http://www.mff.org/publications/publications.taf?page=111*

Paulesu, E., J. and F. Demonet, F. Fazio, E. McCrory, V. Chanoine, N. Brunswick, S. F. Cappa, G. Cossu, M. Habib, C. D. Frith, U. Frith. 2001. "Dyslexia: Cultural Diversity and Biological Unity" *Science.* Vol. 291. No. 551. March 16, 2001.

Peters, Margaret L. 1985. *Spelling: Caught or Taught?* London: Routledge & Kegan Paul.

Piaget, Jean. 1952. *The Origins of Intelligence in Children.* New York: Norton.

Piaget, Jean. 1969. *The Psychology of the Child.* New York: Basic Books.

Reading/English Language Arts: South Carolina Curriculum Standards. 1998. South Carolina Department of Education, Columbia, SC.

Report of the National Reading Panel. 2000. Teaching Children to Read: An Evidence-Based Assessment of the Scientific Research Literature on Reading and Its Implications for Reading Instruction. Washington, DC: National Institute of Child Health and Human Development.

Report of the National Reading Panel: Reports of the Subgroups. 2000. Washington, DC: U.S. Department of Health and Human Services.

Richgels, D. 1995. "Invented Spelling Ability and Printed Word Learning in Kindergarten." *Reading Research Quarterly* 30 (1), 96-109.

_____ 1987. "Experimental Reading with Invented Spelling (ERIS): A Preschool and Kindergarten Method." *The Reading Teacher*, 40, 522-529.

Ryder, R. J. and M. F. Graves. 1994. "Vocabulary Instruction Presented Prior to Reading in Two Basal Readers." *Elementary School Journal*, 95(2), 139-153.

Schultz, Christine. 2001. "Why We Love Love." *Attaché*. Greensboro, NC: Attaché, Pace Communications, Inc. (February, pp. 61-64).

Scott, J. and Linnea Ehri. 1990. "Sight word reading in prereaders; Use of logographic vs. alphabetic access routes." *Journal of Reading Behavior*, 22, 149-166.

Shanahan, Timothy. 1997. "Reading-Writing Relationships, Thematic Units, Inquiry Learning...In Pursuit of Effective Integrated Literacy Instruction." *The Reading Teacher*, 51 (1): 12-19.

Smith, Frank. 1988. *Joining the Literacy Club*. Portsmouth, NH: Heinemann.

Stauffer, Russell. 1969. *Directing Reading Maturity as a Cognitive Process*. NY: Harper & Row.

_____ 1968. "Reading Is a Cognitive Process." *Elementary English*, 44, 348.

Stoll, Clifford. 1995. *Silicon Snake Oil: Second Thoughts on the Information Highway*. NY: Anchor Books.

Taylor, B. M. and B. J. Fry, G. M. Maruyama. 1990. "Time Spent Reading and Reading Growth." *American Educational Research Journal*, 27 (#2 Summer), 351-362.

West Virginia Instructional Goals and Objectives. 2000. West Virginia Department of Education. *http://wvde.state.wv.us/igos/new.html*

Yates, Elizabeth. 1995. *Someday You'll Write*. Greenville, SC: Bob Jones University Press.

Zutell, J. 1998. "Word Sorting: A Developmental Spelling Approach to Word Study for Delayed Readers." *Reading and Writing Quarterly*, 14, #2, April - June, 219-238.

ACKNOWLEDGMENTS
(continued)

Excerpt from *Out of Africa* by Isak Dinesen, copyright 1937, 1938 by Random House, Inc., copyright renewed 1965 by Rungstedlundfonden, reprinted by permission of Random House, Inc.

Text and illustration reproduced from *Cat on the Mat* by Brian Wildsmith, by permission of Oxford University Press.

Learning to Spell: Research, Theory and Practice Across Languages by Perfetti, Reiben and Fayol. 1997. Permission granted by Lawrence Erlbaum Associates and Linnea C. Ehri

Guiding Readers and Writers Grades 3–6 by Fountas and Pinnell, © 2001. Heinemann.

Mosaic of Thought by Keene and Zimmermann, © 1997. Heinemann.

Reprinted by permission of the publisher from *Playing in the Dark* by Toni Morrison, p. xi, Cambridge, Mass.: Harvard University Press, Copyright © 1992 by Toni Morrison.

Reprinted by permission of the publishers from *The Letters of Emily Dickinson* edited by Thomas H. Johnson, Cambridge, Mass.: The Belknap Press of Harvard University Press, Copyright © 1958, 1986 by the President and Fellows of Harvard College.

Computers/Technology Skills Curriculum 1998 provided with permission from the Public Schools of North Carolina.

From *The Great Fire* by Jim Murphy. Copyright © 1995 by Jim Murphy. Reprinted by permission of Scholastic, Inc.

Used with permission from Carson-Dellosa Publishing Company, CD-2407 *Guided Reading the Four-Blocks™ Way*.

From *When Pigasso Met Mootisse* by Nina Laden. Copyright ©1998 by Nina Laden. Published by Chronicle Books.

Reprinted from *My Kid Can't Spell! Understanding and Assisting your Child's Literacy Development* by J. Richard Gentry. Copyright © 1997 by J. Richard Gentry. Published by Heinemann, a division of Reed Elsevier Inc., Portsmouth, NH. Reprinted by permission of the publisher.

Excerpt from *Roll of Thunder,* by Mildred Taylor. Text © Mildred Taylor, 1976. Puffin Books.

NOTES

NOTES

NOTES